This book is dedicated to my

wonderful sister, Aurora.

Thank you for encouragement.

CONTENT

Drawing and Painting are two types

of fine arts with many differences

between them.

Drawing is the basis of painting

and the converse is not true.

You should be a good at drawing

if you want to excel as a painter.

Audrey Heburn, pencil drawing on,

Stainbach paper

by Victoria Sara Dazin

Pencils:HB,4B,6B,7B,9B

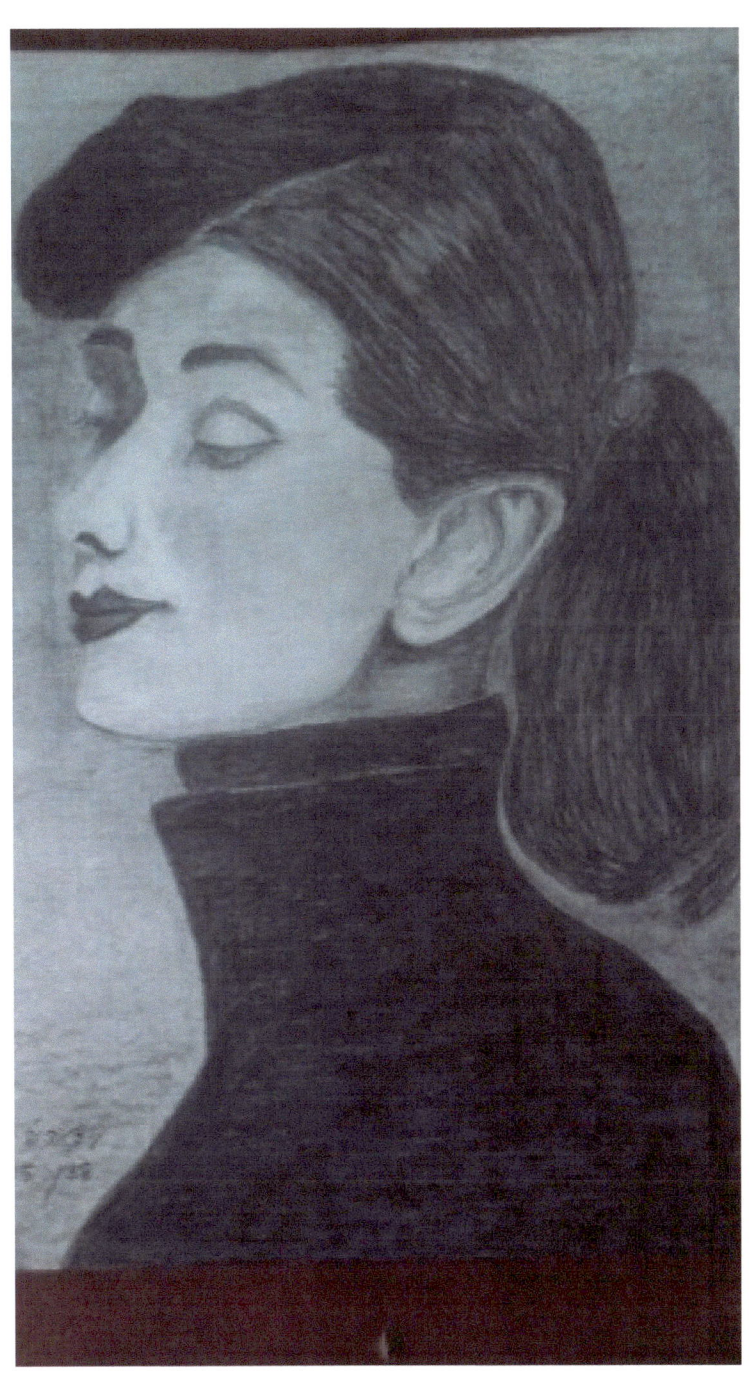

The terminology also differs in the

case of drawing and painting.

A person who draws is called

an artist whereas

a person who paints is called either

an artist or a painter.

Ballerina by Victoria Sara Dazin

Aquarelle on Saunders paper,

56/46 cm.

Inspired by "Purity" of Andrew
Atroshenko

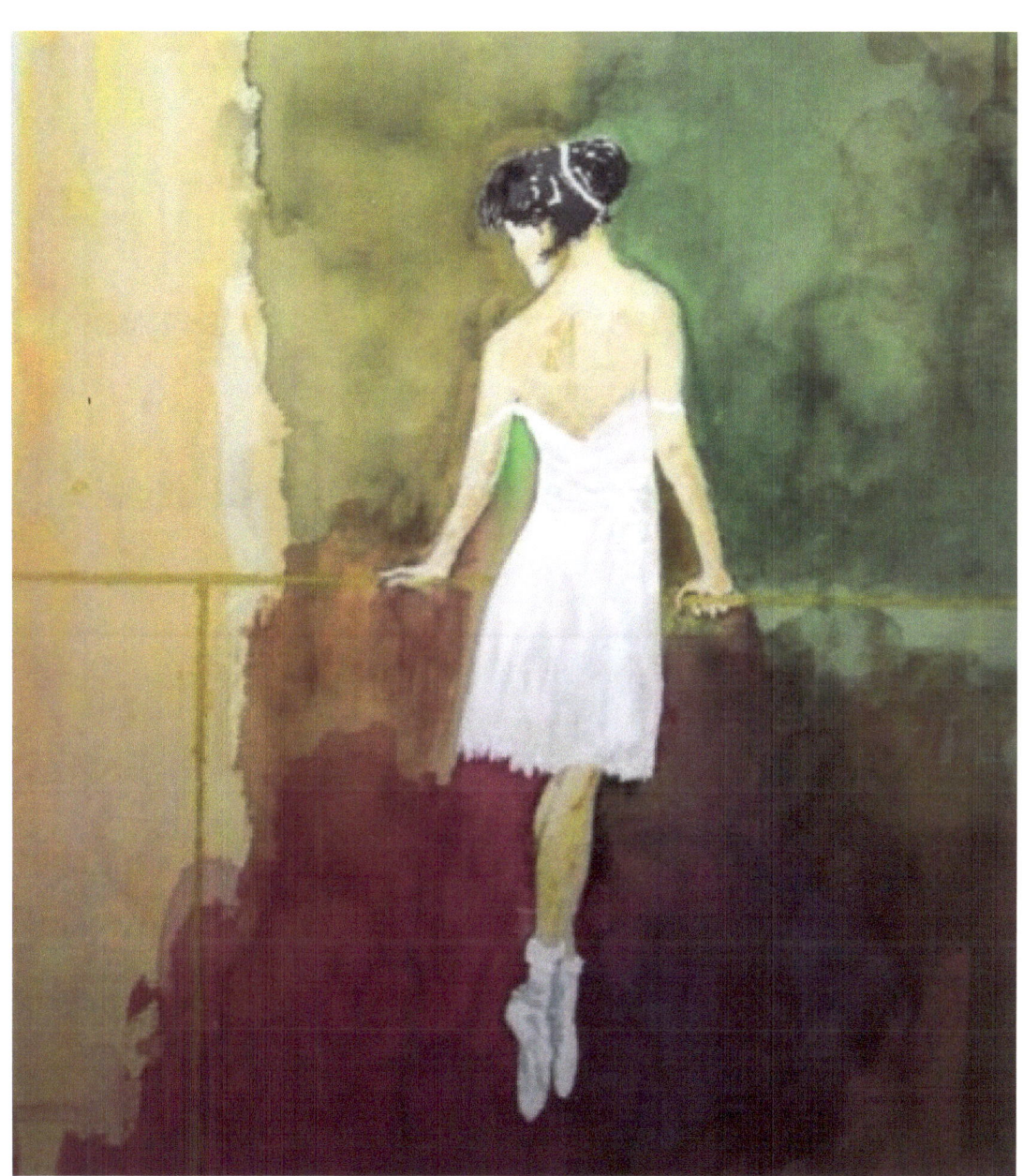

It is also a market value for both drawing and painting works.

Works of painting generally have a greater market value than the works of pencil and charcoal drawing.

Norma Shearer, 1920. By Victoria Sara Dazin

Carbon drawing on Steinbach paper, 70/50 cm

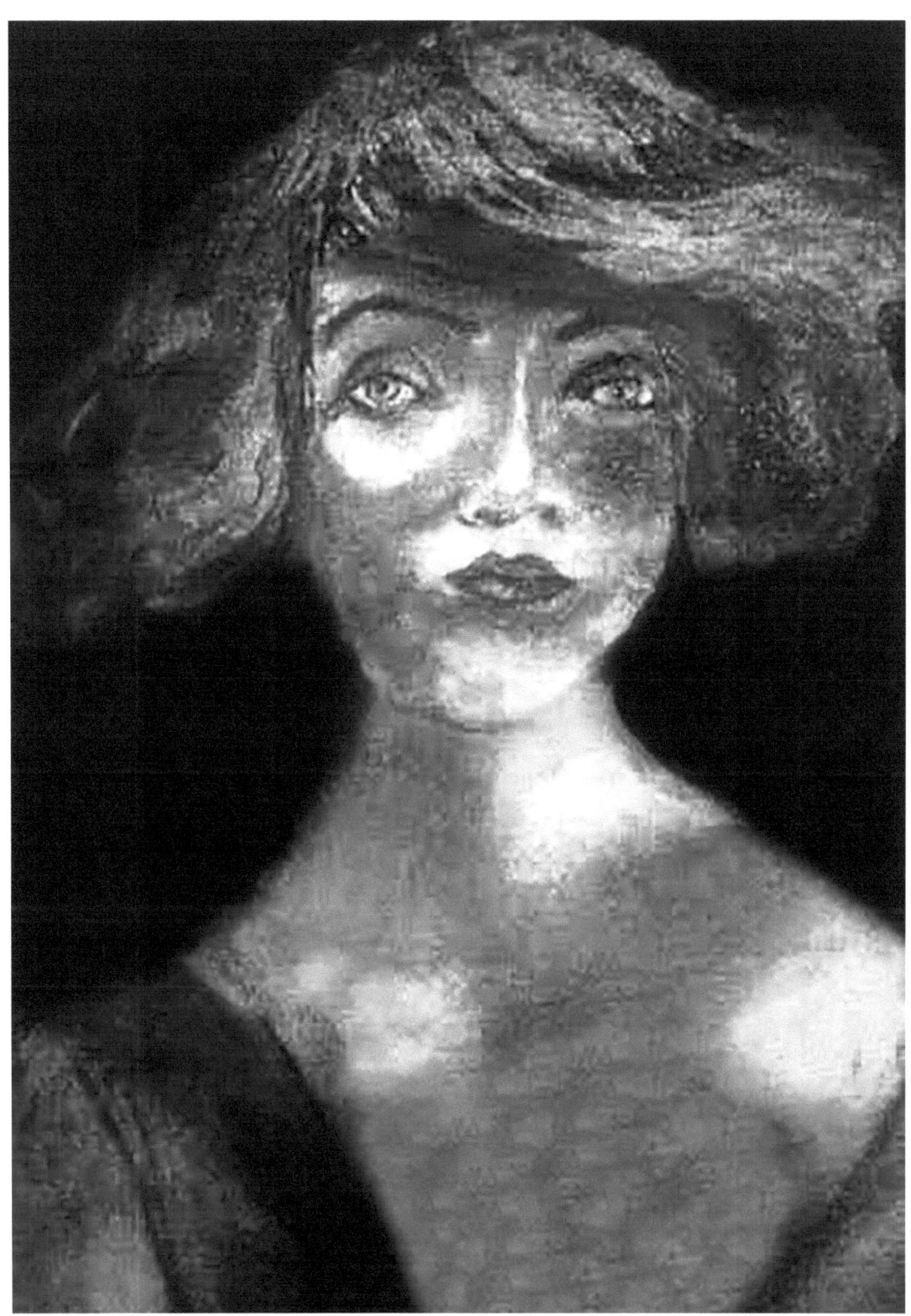

The painting equipment is generally expensive to buy when compared to drawing equipment.

Woman on summer by Victoria Sara Dazin, aquarelle 56/46cm on Saunders paper.

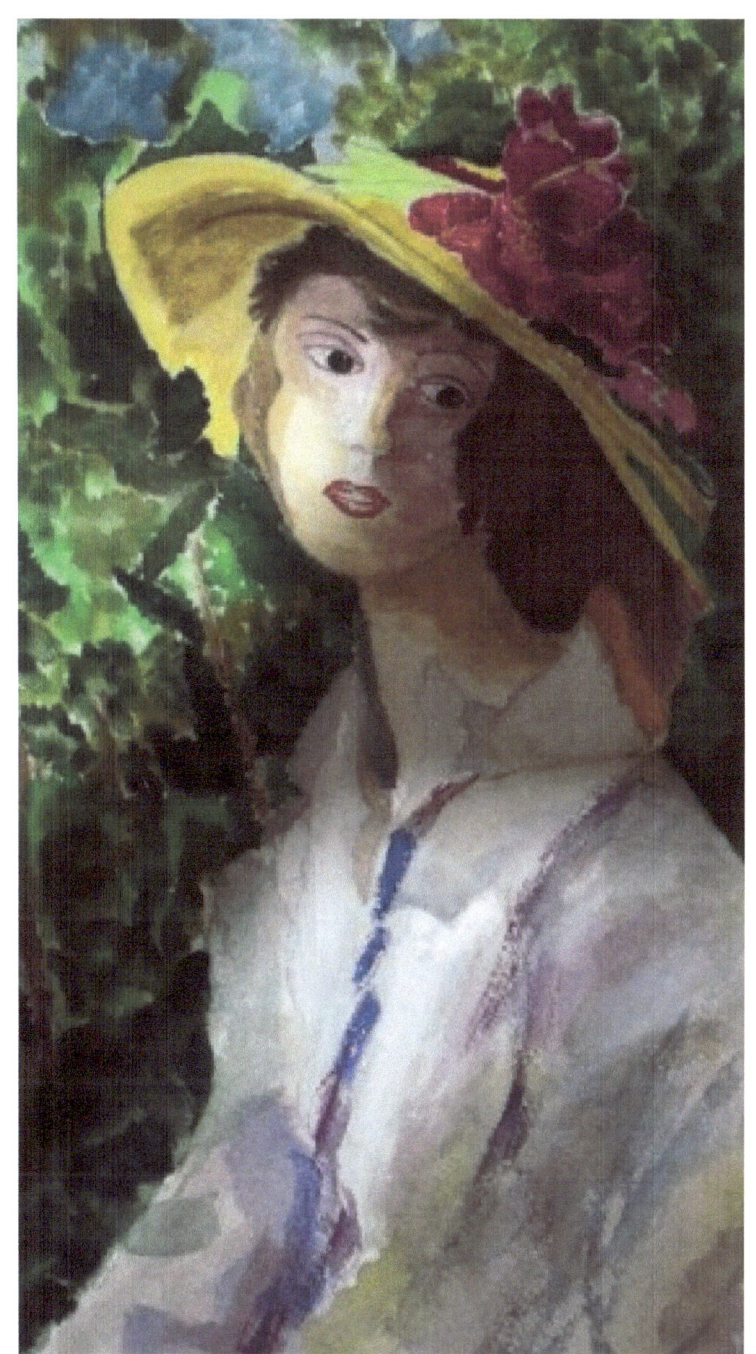

Drawing is characterized by lines and shades. Drawing is of different types such as line drawing, shade drawing and object drawing.

Pencil, crayons and charcoal can be .used in the art of drawing.

Blue eyes woman- pencil drawing on Steinbach paper, 46/36 cm.

by Victoria Sara Dazin . Pencils: HB,4HB,6HB

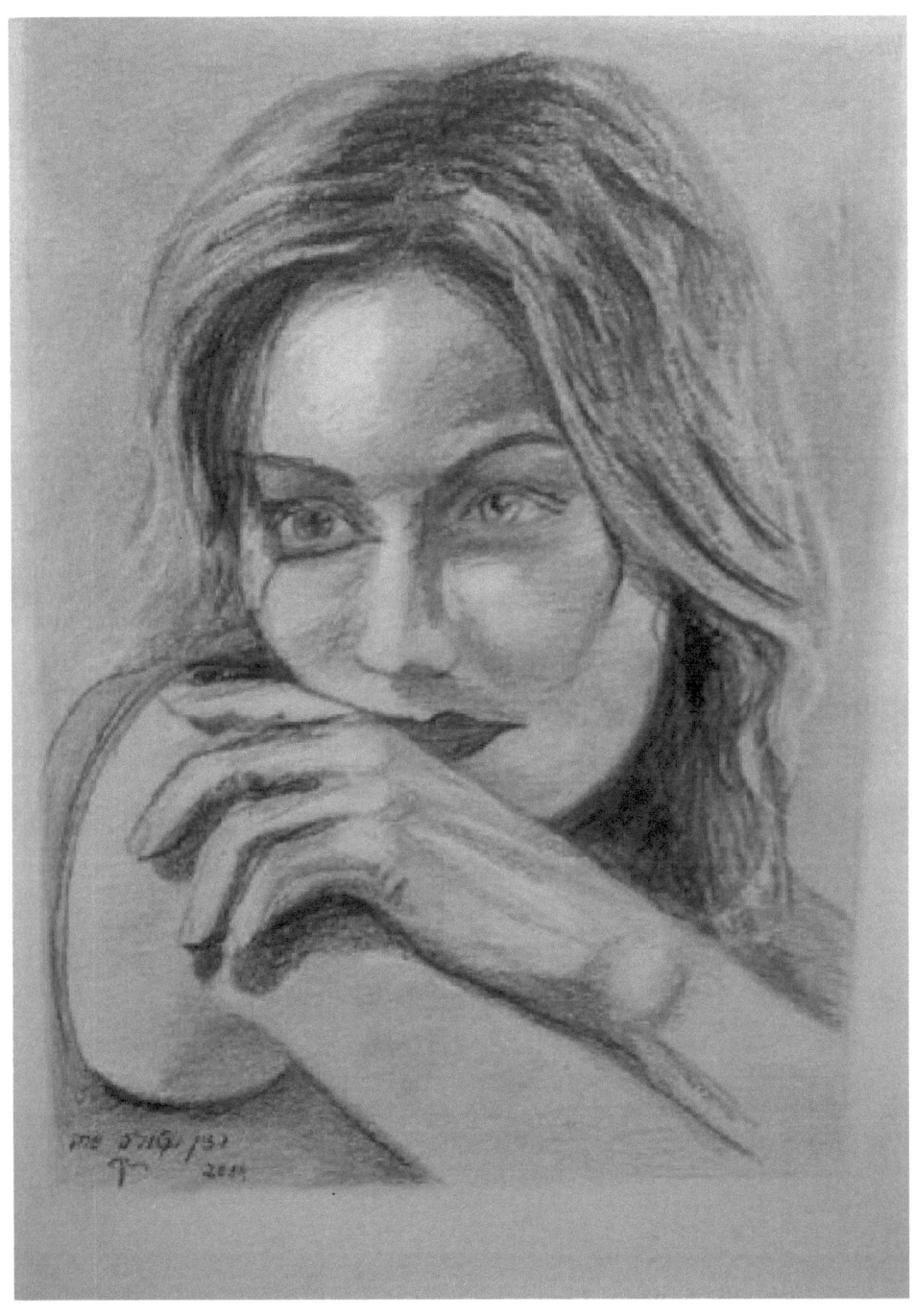

Woman portrait, carbon drawing

by Victoria Sara Dazin

on Stainbach paper, 46/36cm.

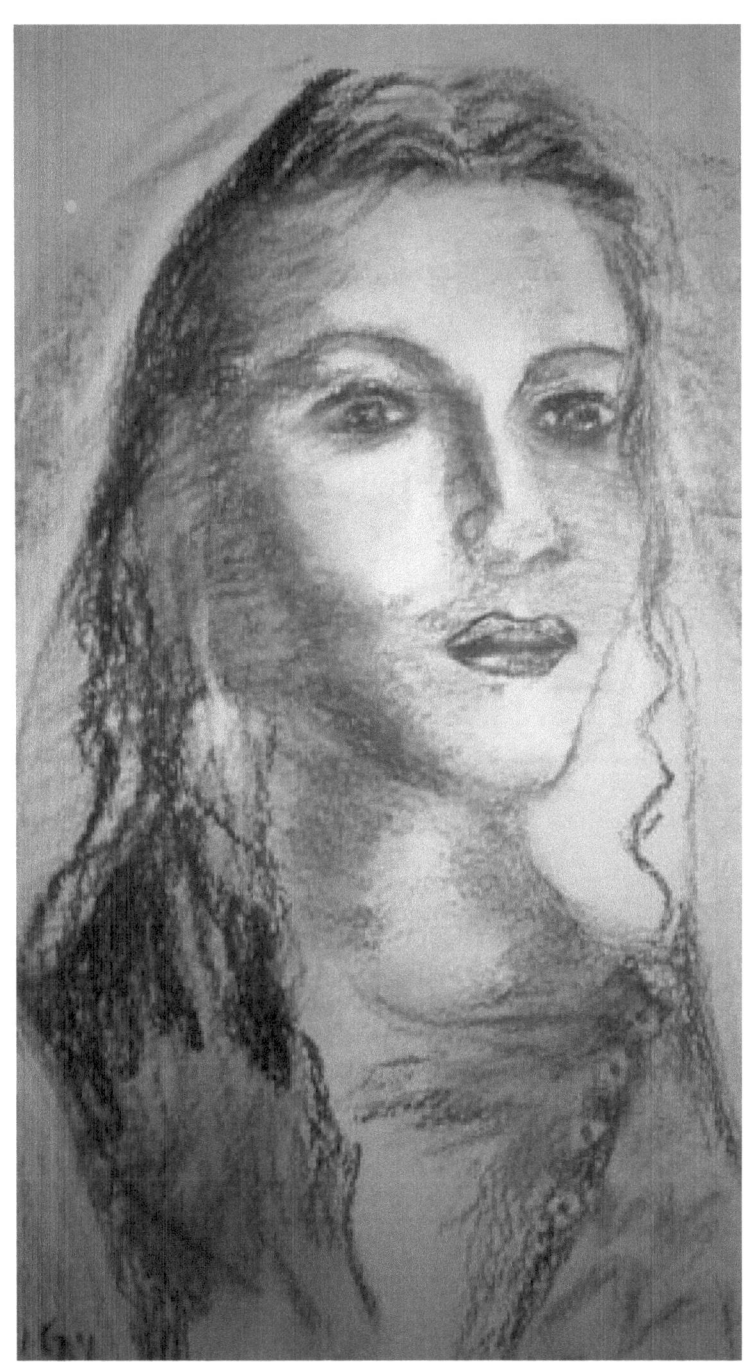

Little girl, pencil drawing on Steinbach
paper, 46/36cm

by Victoria Sara Dazin

Pencils: HB,4HB,6HB

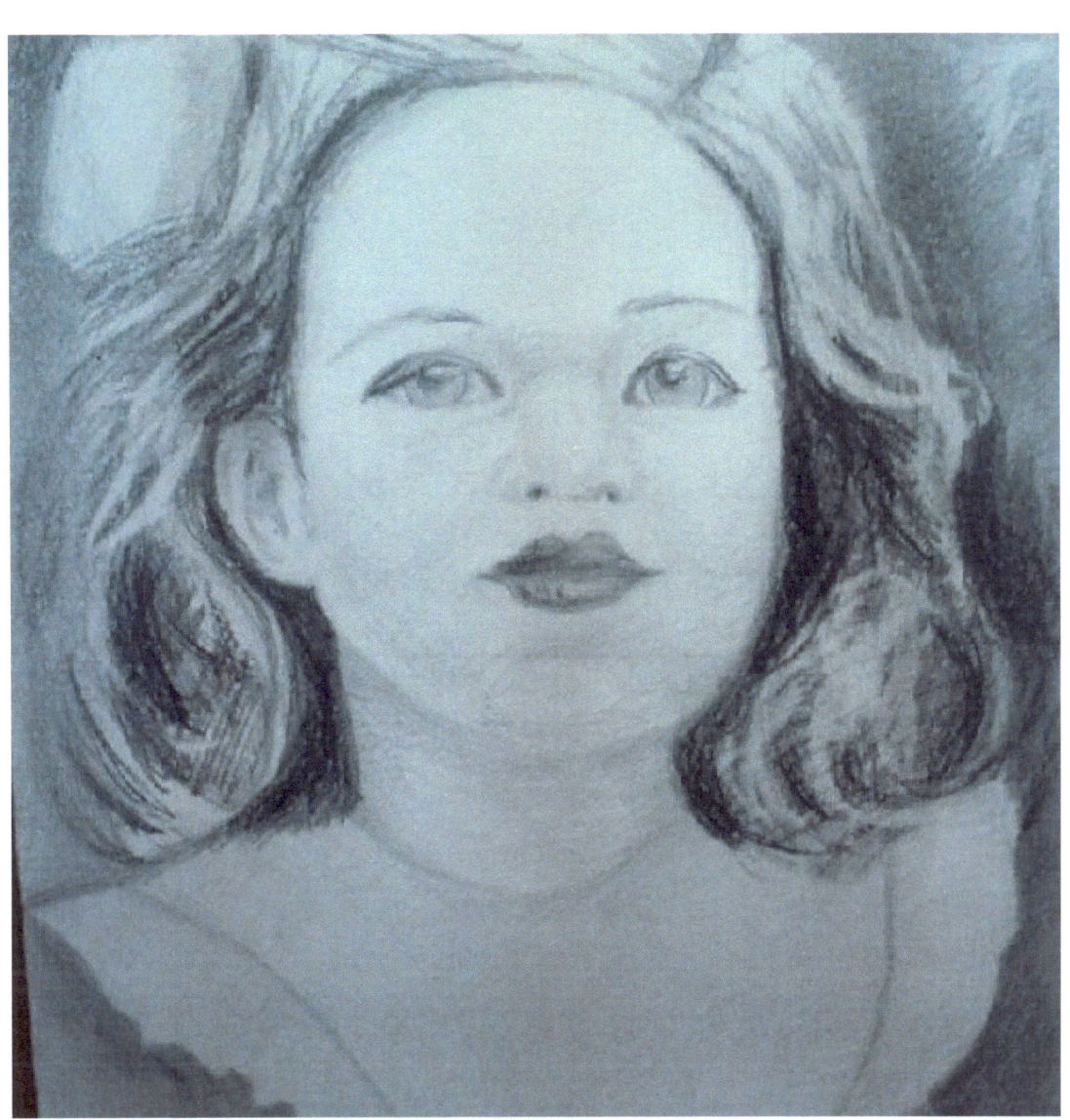

American Native - an Acoma Pueblo woman , pencil drawing on Steinbach paper, 46/36cm

by Victoria Sara Dazin

Pencils: HB, 4HB, 6HB

American Native – an Acoma Pueblo woman

A sailor man , pencil drawing on Steinbach paper , 46/36cm.

by Victoria Sara Dazin

Pencils: HB,4HB,6HB.

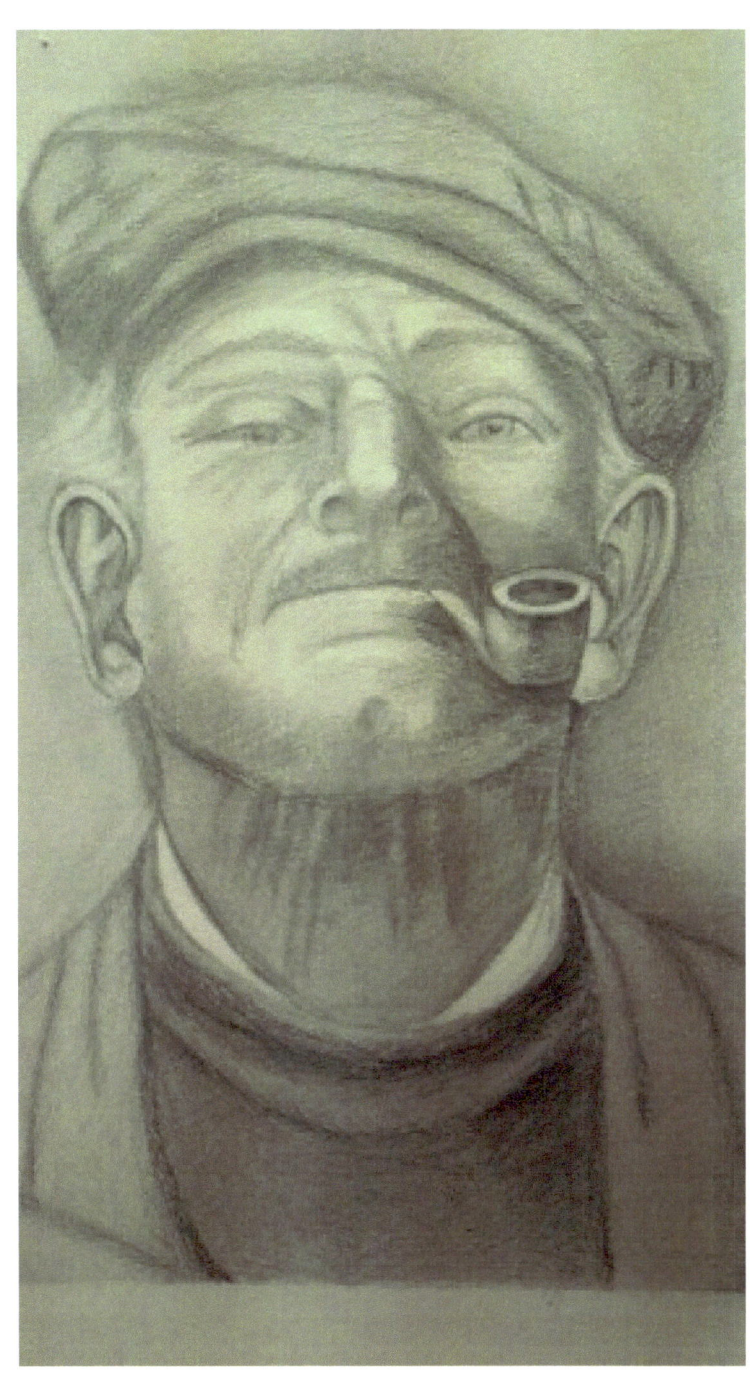

A boy , pencil drawing on Steinbach

Paper, 46/36cm

by Victoria Sara Dazin

Pencils: HB,4HB,6HB

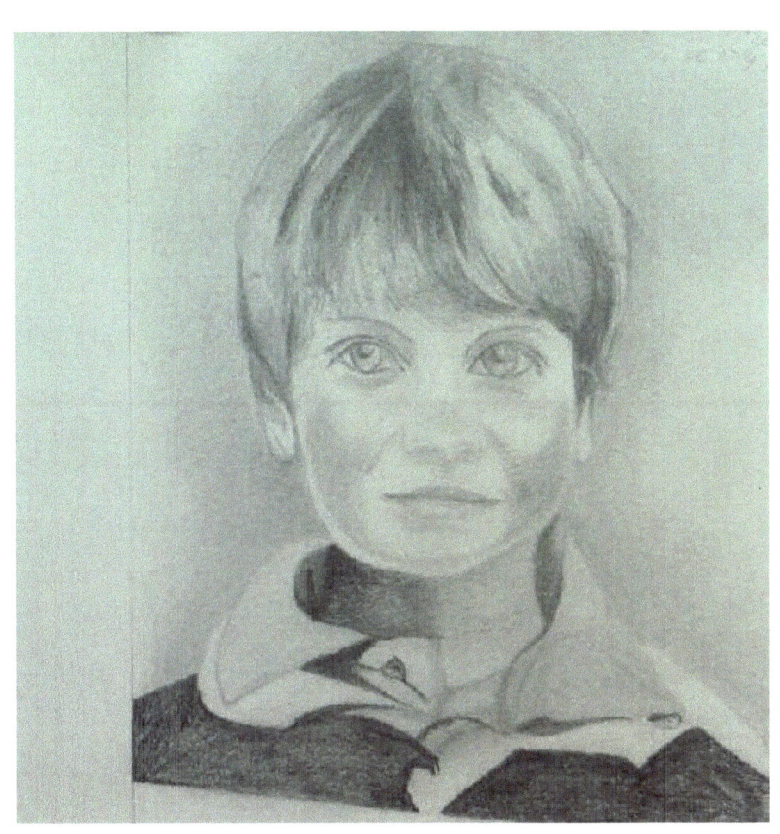

A man, carbon drawing on Steinbach
paper,46/36cm

by Victoria Sara Dazin

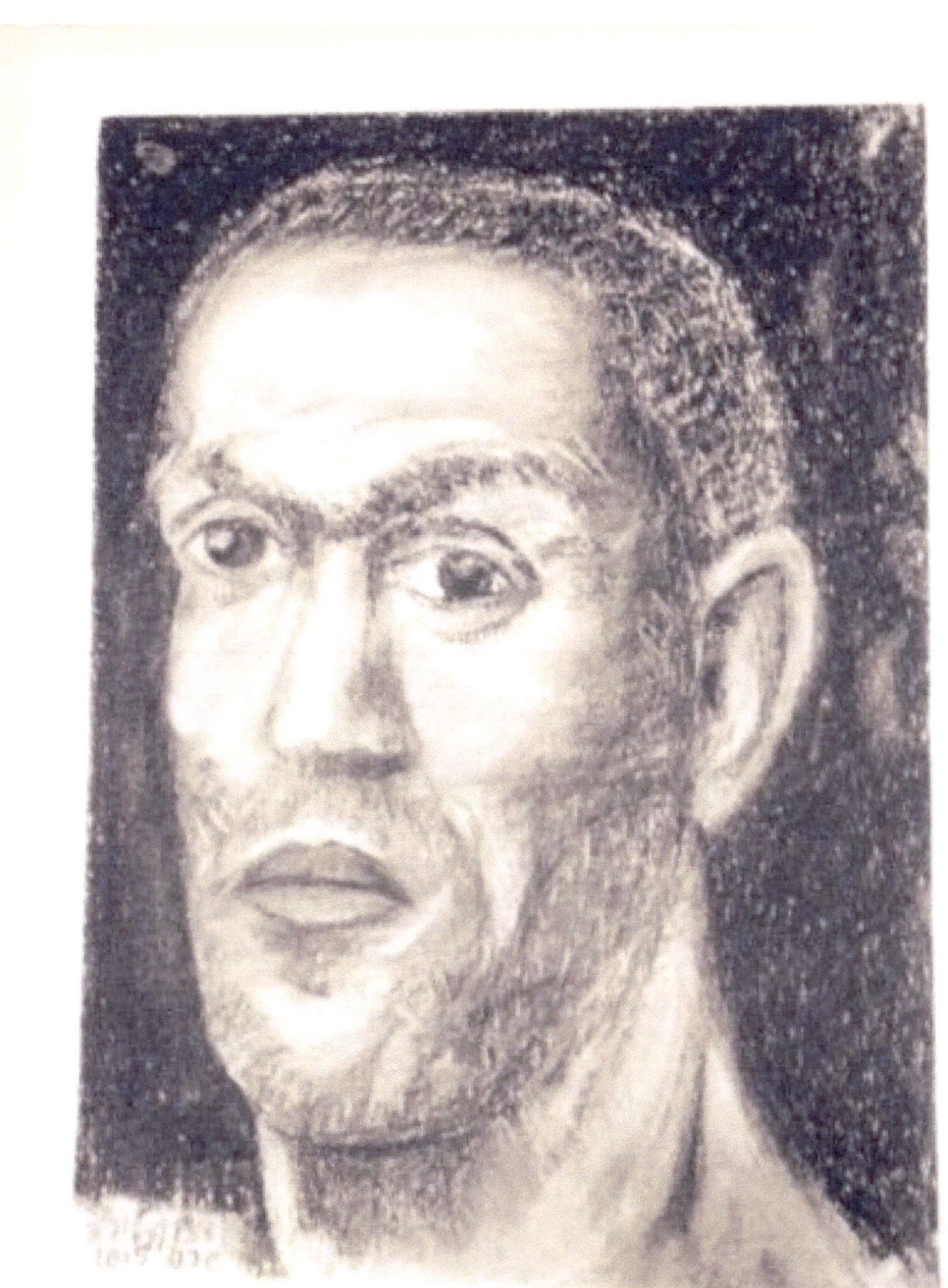

Pencil drawing inspired by

Michelangelo, 46/36 cm

cm, by Victoria Sara Dazin , on

Steinbach paper.

Pencils: HB,4HB,6HB

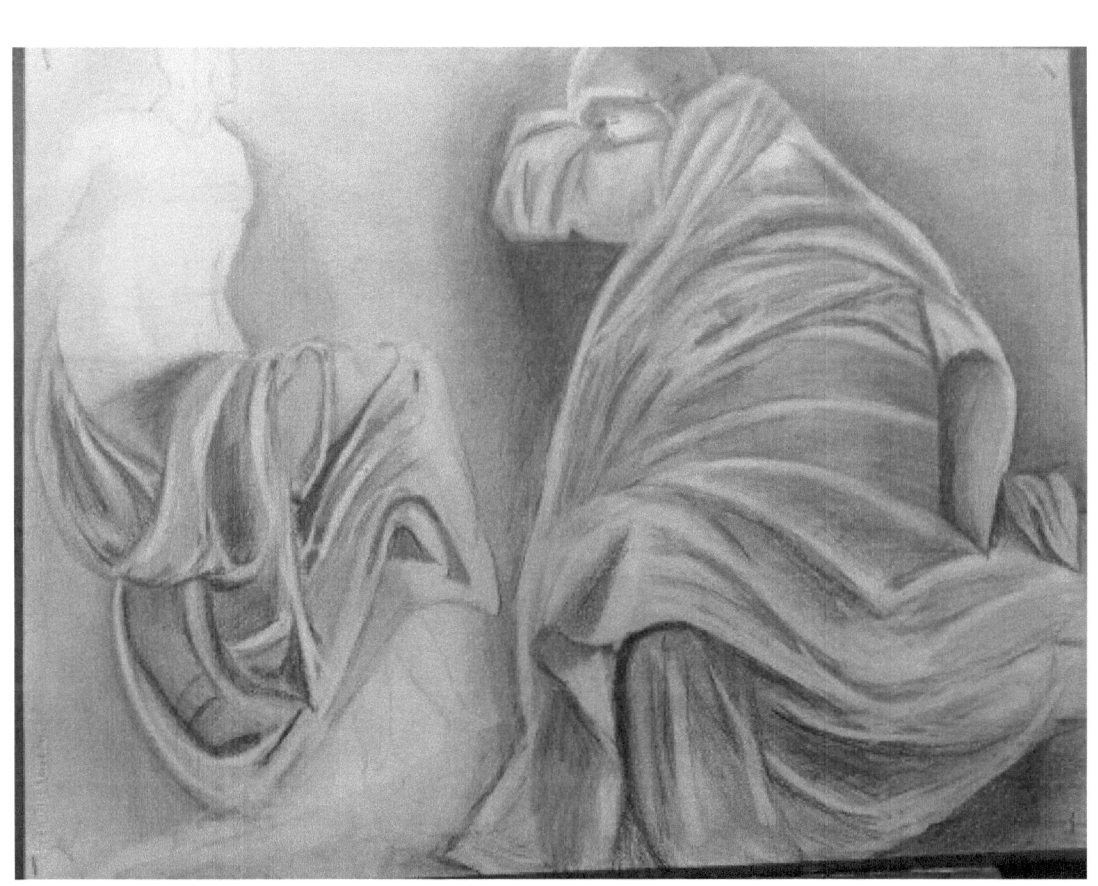

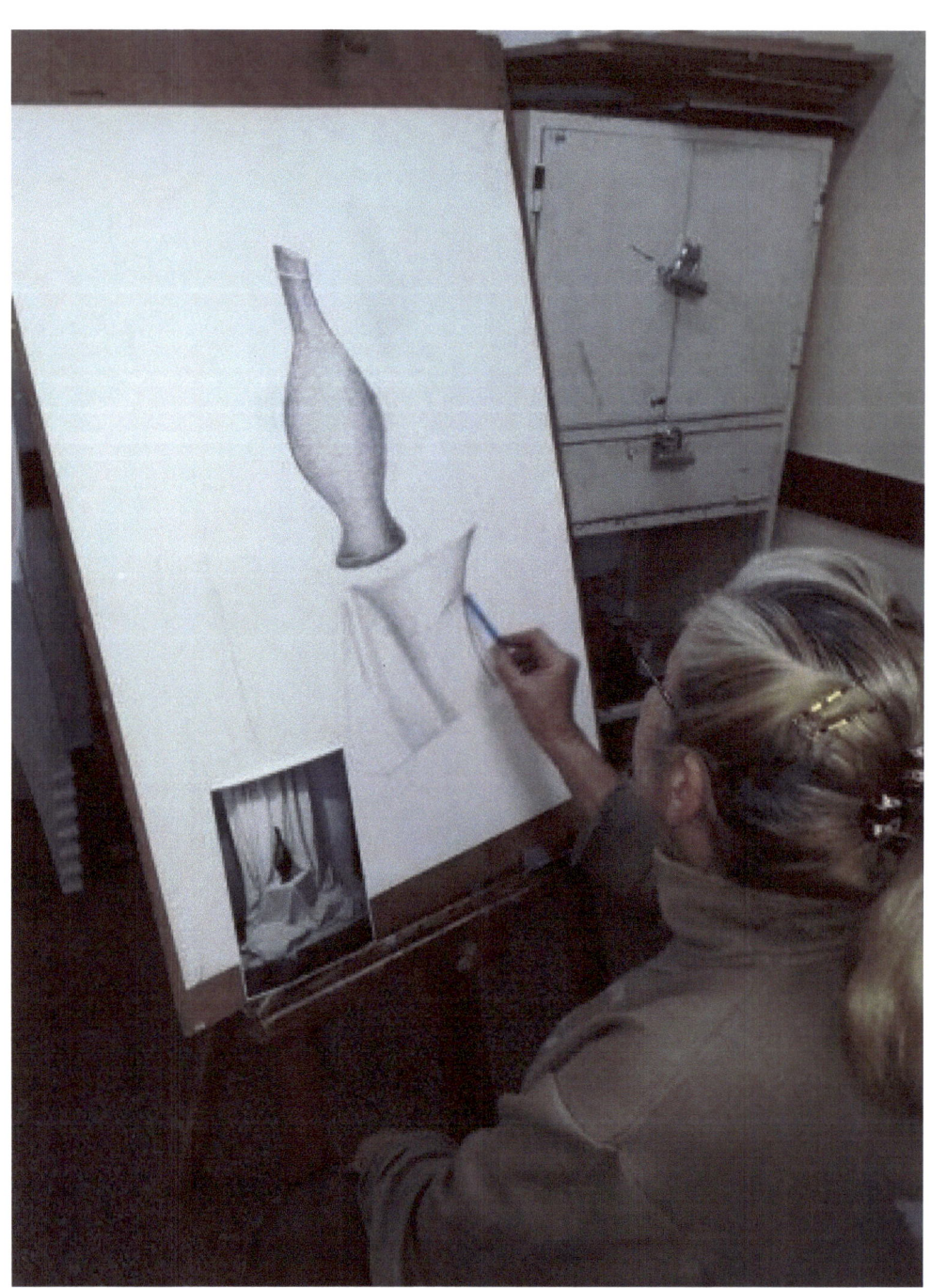

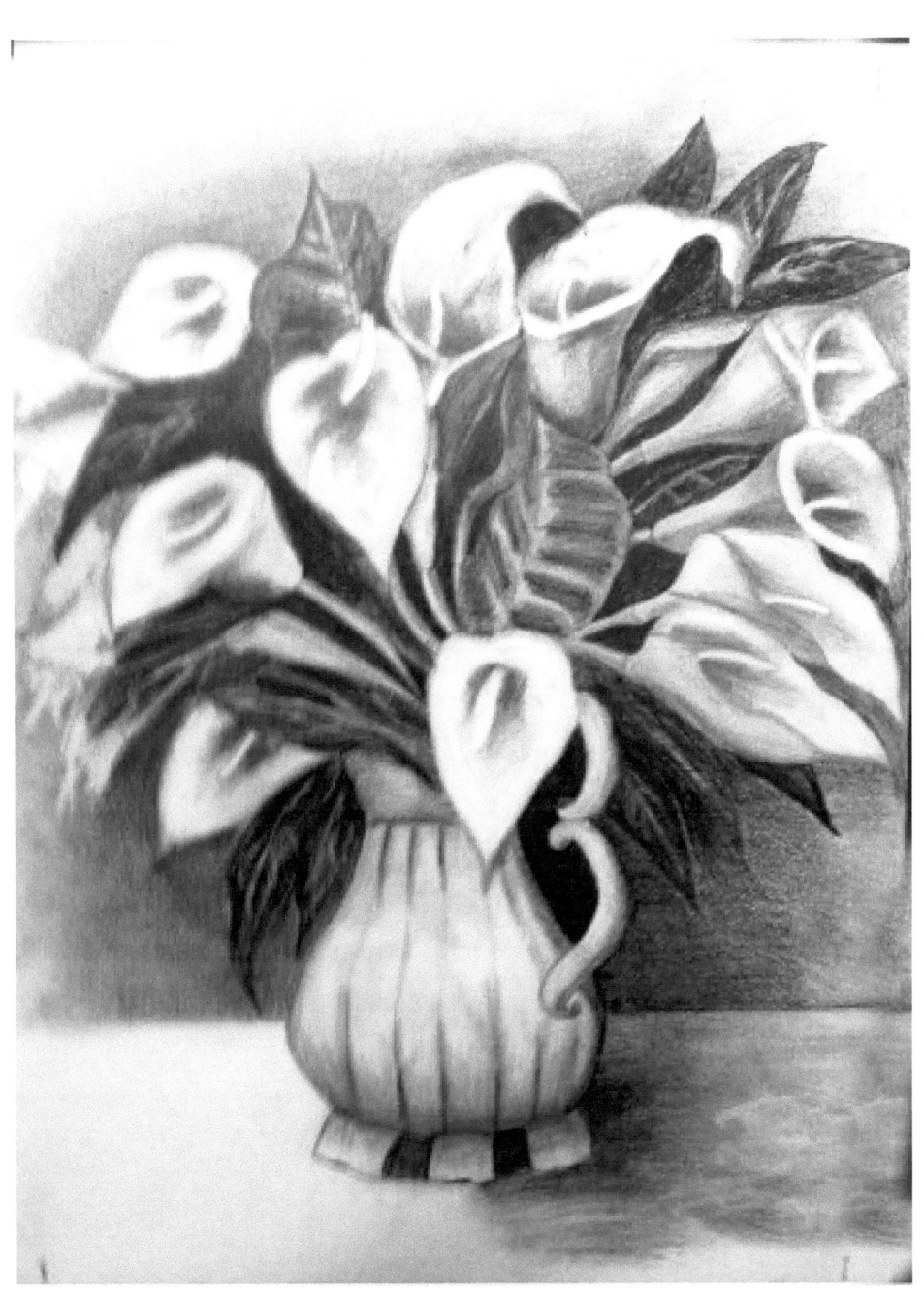

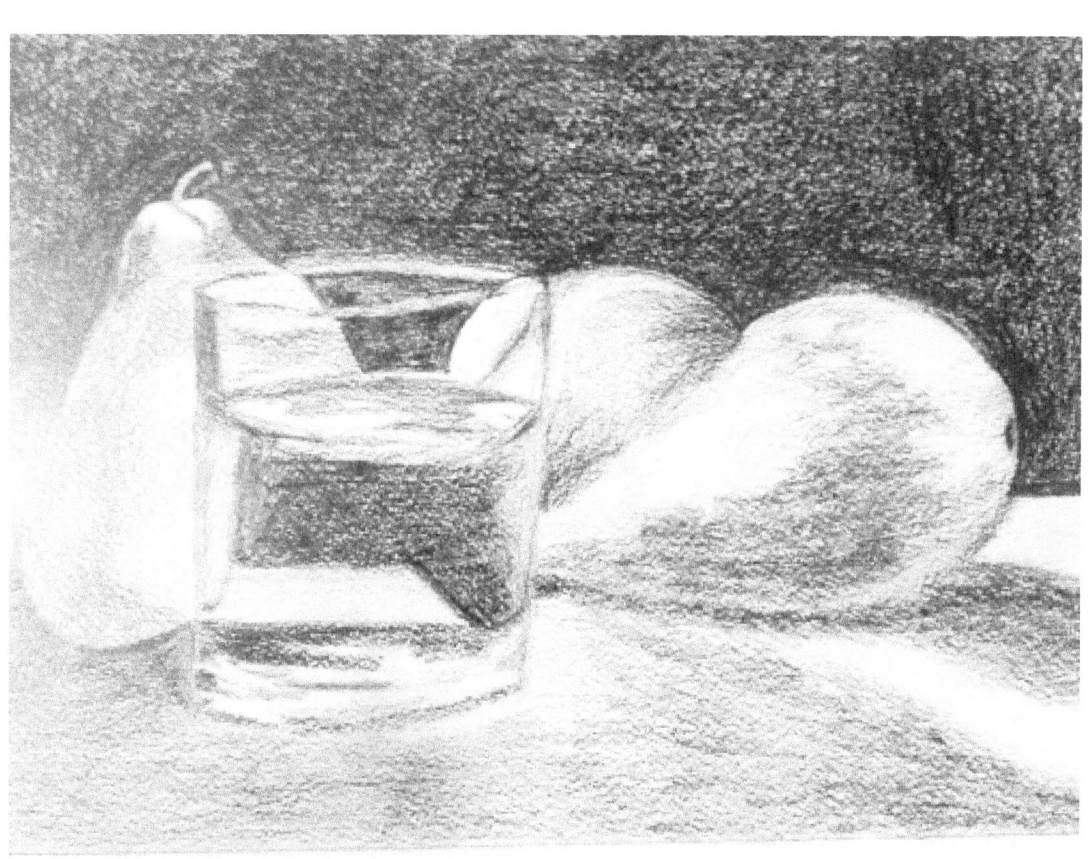

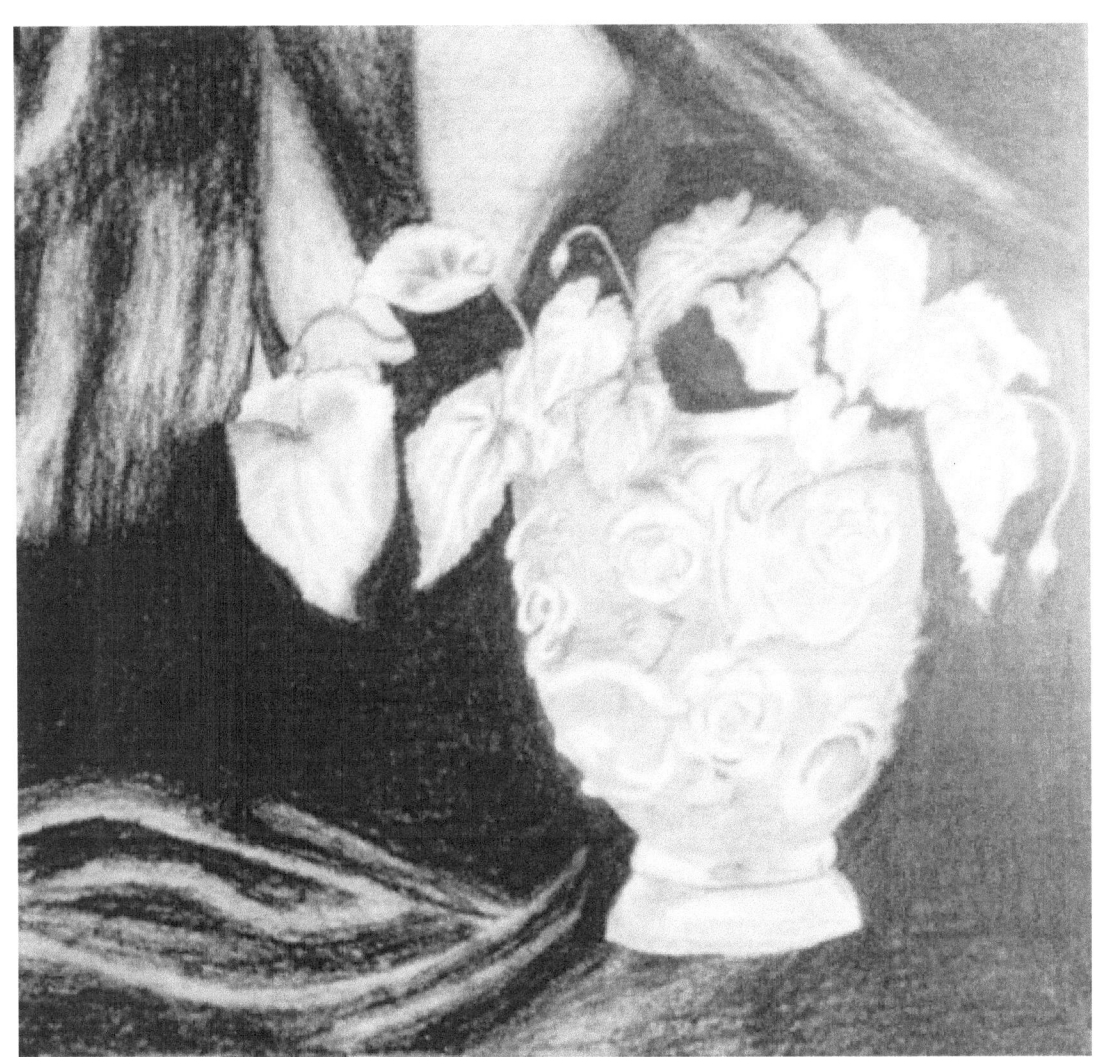

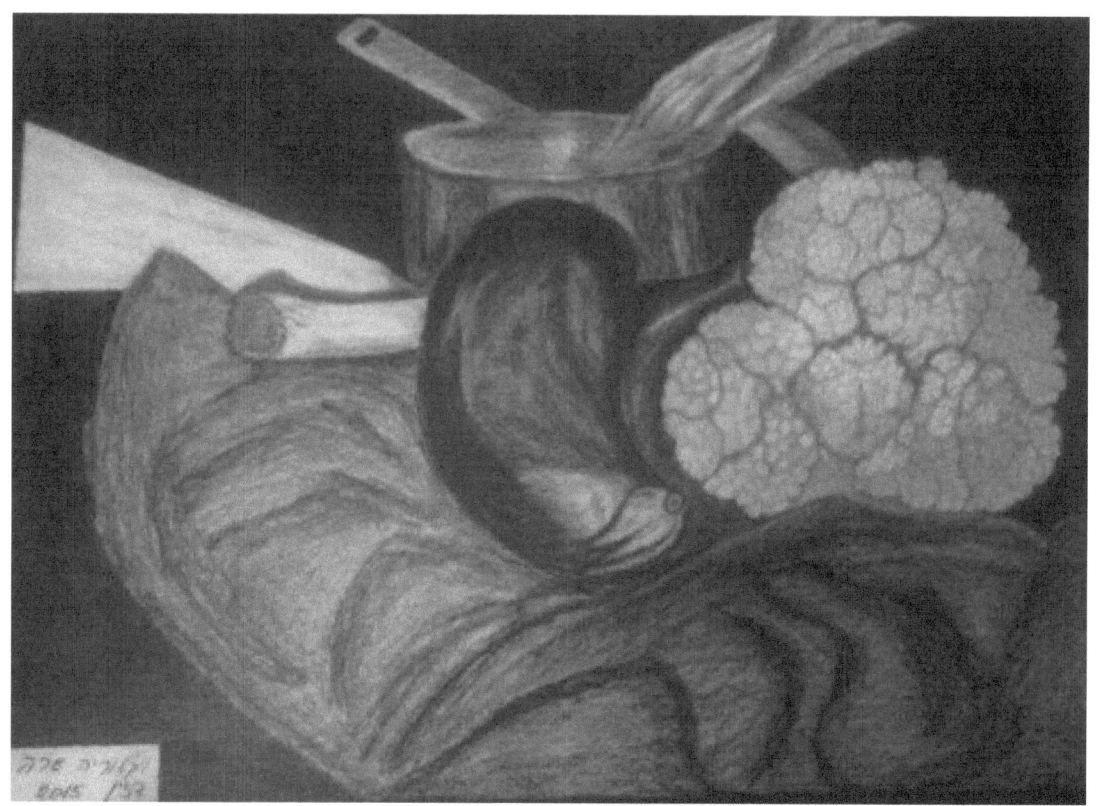

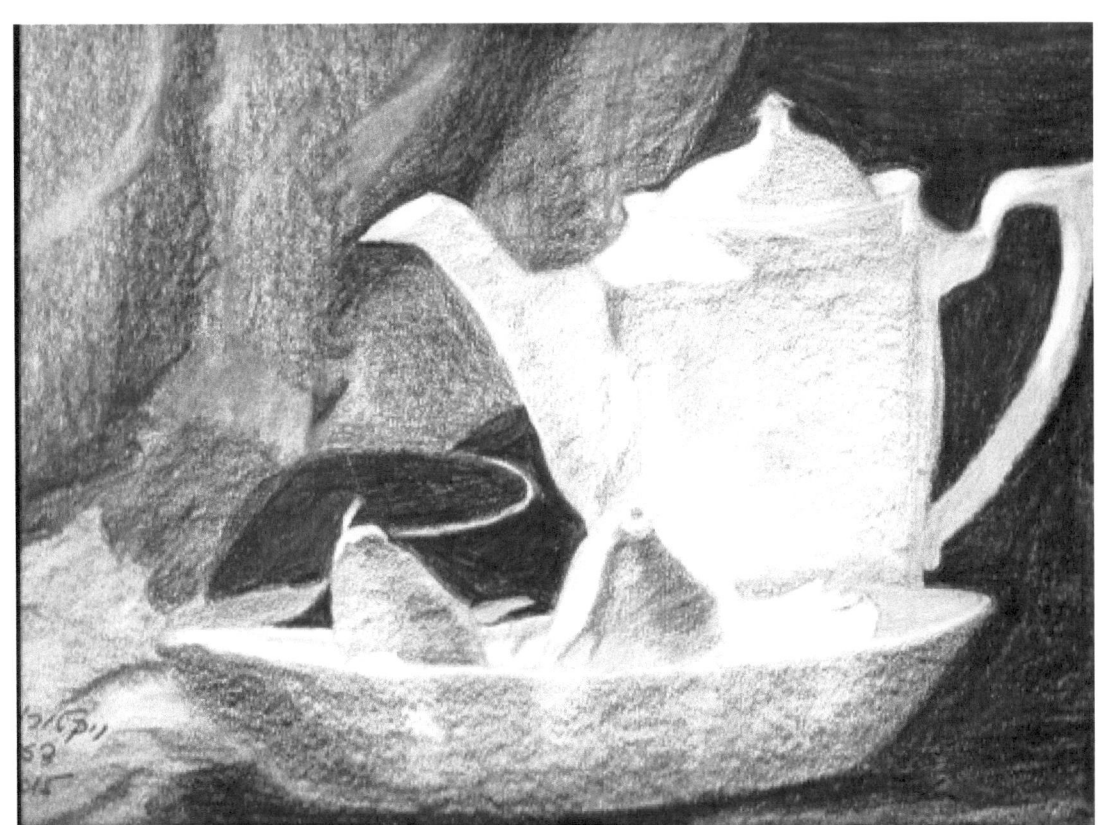

Japan geisha - colours pencils drawing

on Steinbach paper,46/36cm.

by Victoria Sara Dazin

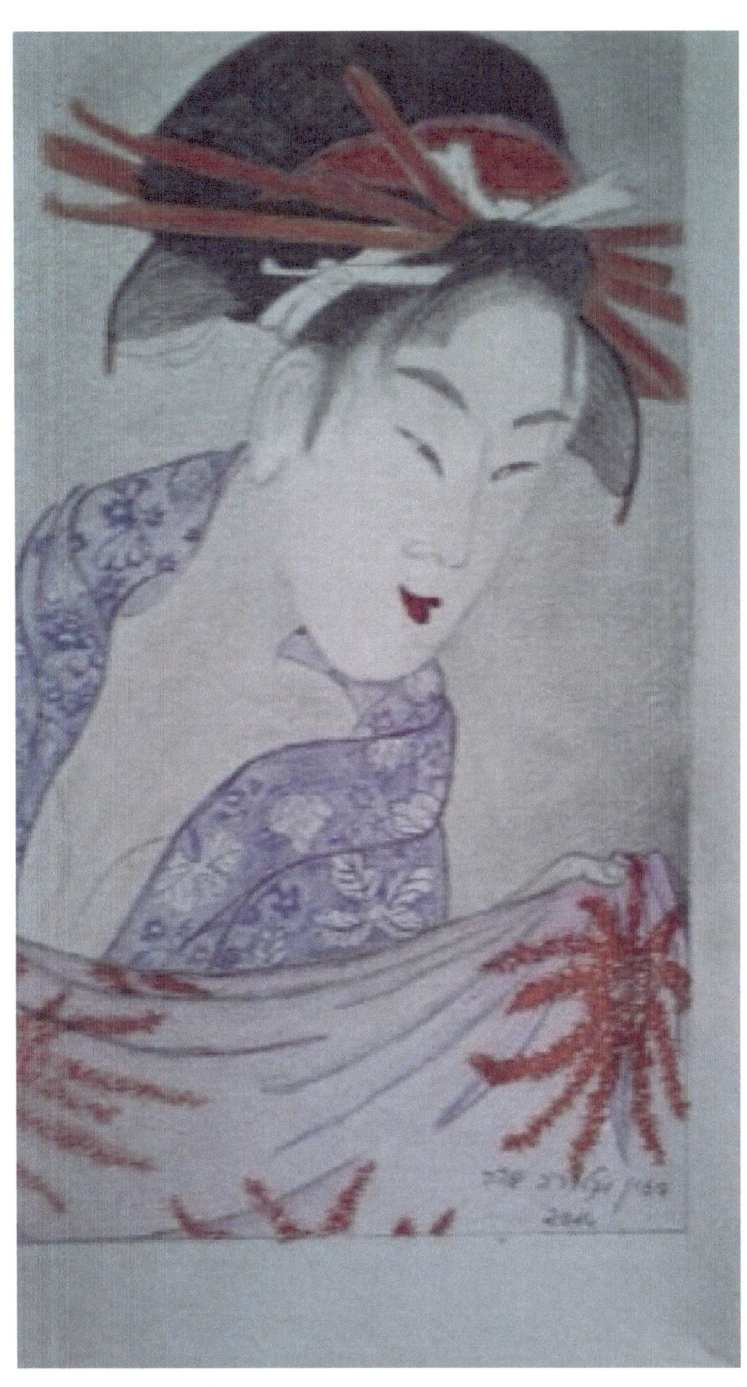

Painting is characterized by colors and designs.

Painting is different types such as, painting on canvas

oil painting on canvas, water color painting, acrylic painting.

A lady with a little dog by Victoria

Sara Dazin .Water color, on Saunders paper, 46/33 cm.

Painting inspired by George Seurat.

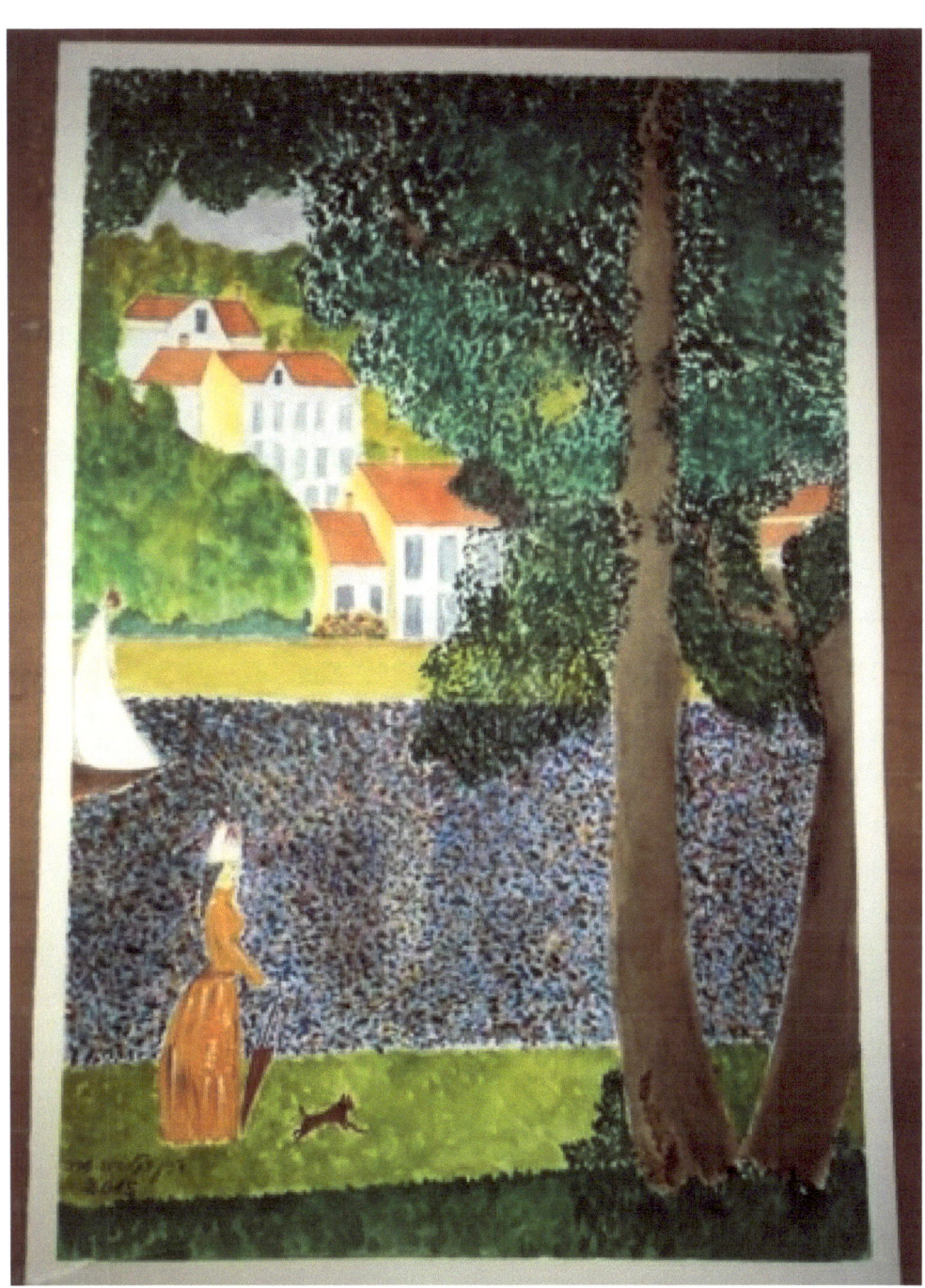

Oil colors, acrylic and types of

pigments are used in

the art of painting.

Tango by Victoria Sara Dazin.

Water color, on Saunders paper

46/36cm

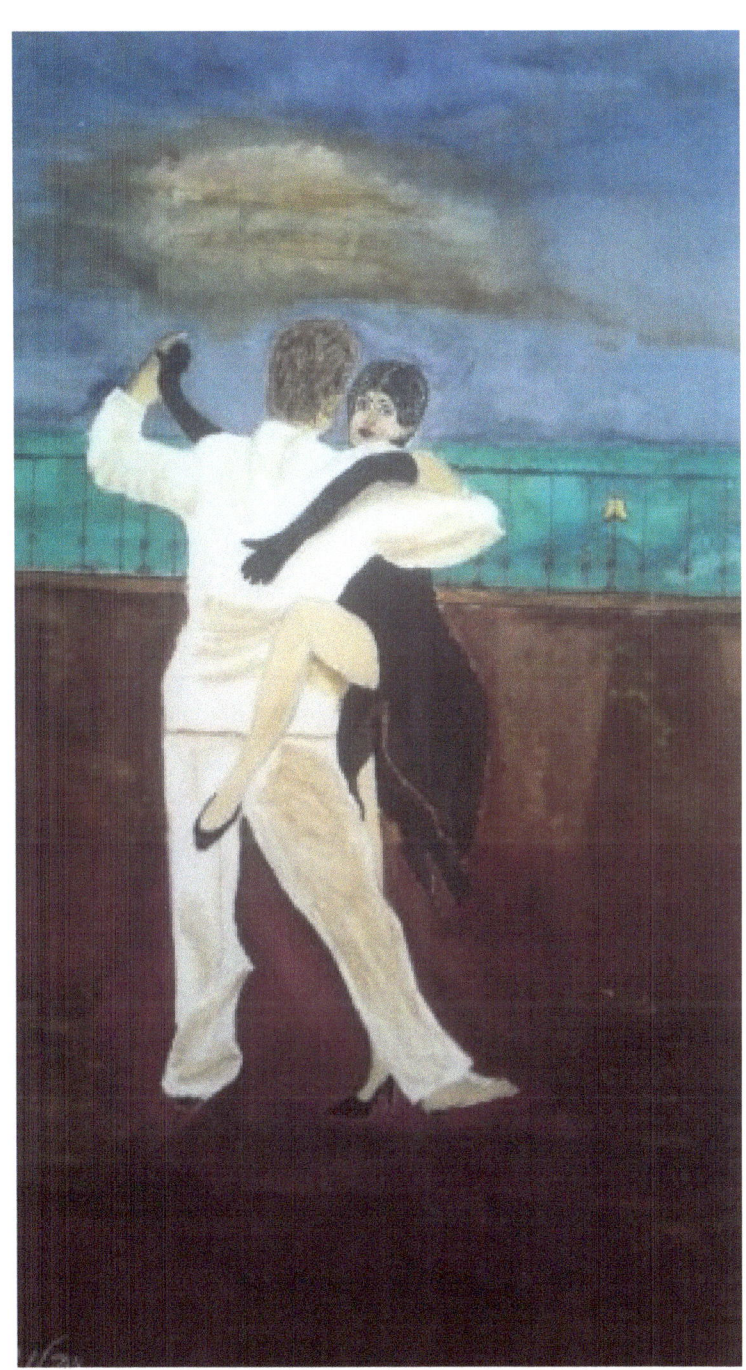

We need to have different kinds

of brushes with different

bristles in the case of painting.

Blue Veil , aquarelle

on Saunders paper, 46/33 cm

by Victoria Sara Dazin.

Inspired by Pablo Picasso – Bust

of Woman

with Blue Veil (Olga), 1924.

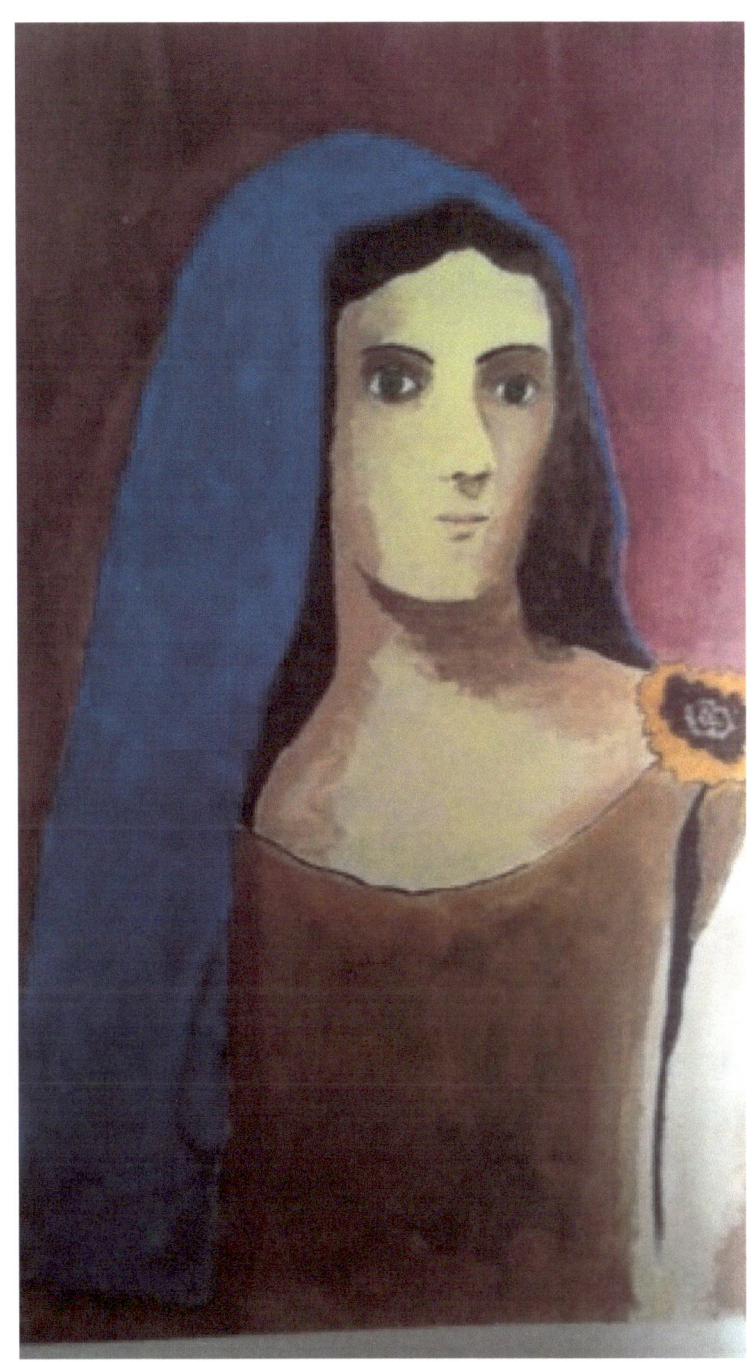

Oil painting and acrylic cannot be
very easily erased or altered.

Astronomia by Victoria Sara Dazin,

on Saunders paper ,water color ,

47/33 cm

Inspired by Sandro Boticelli

"Giovano introduto tra

le Arti Liberali" 1481 .(Detail)

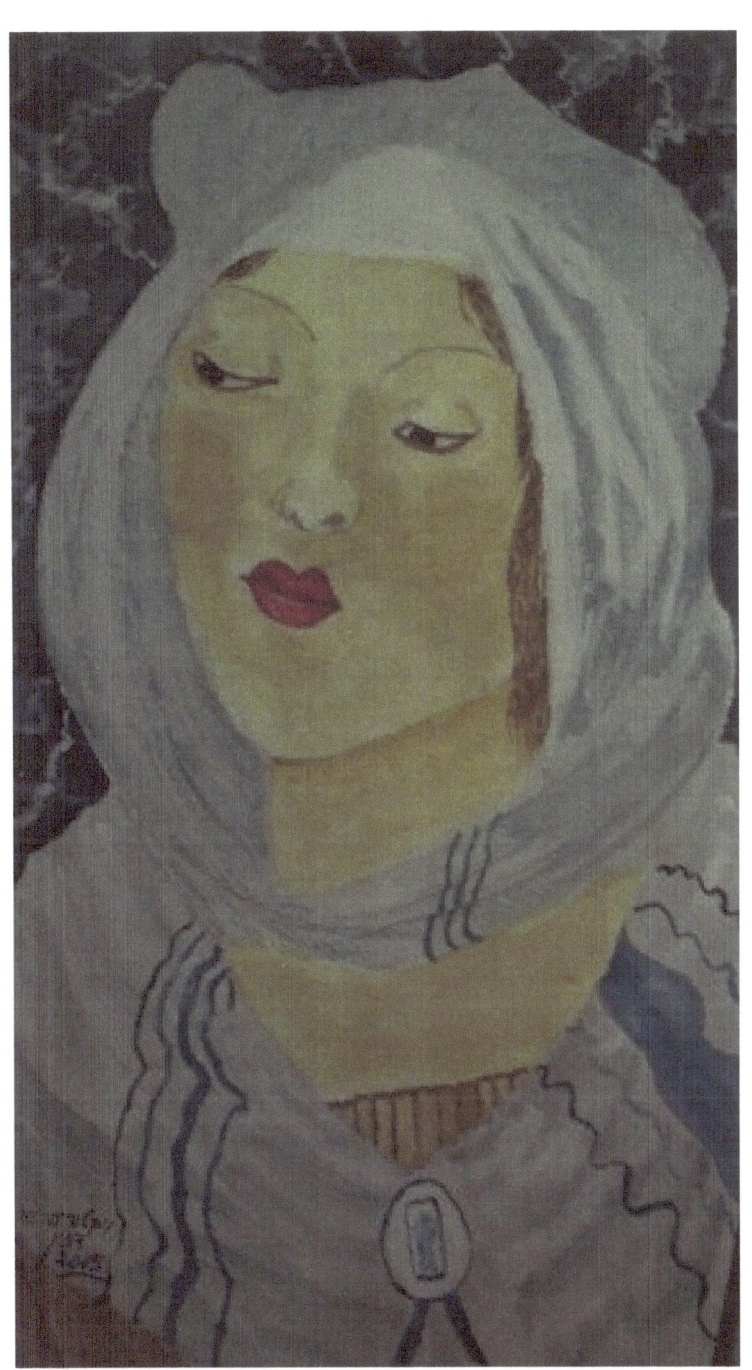

The painting equipment is generally expensive to buy when compared to drawing equipment.

Contessa Alexandra Pavlovna –

aquarelle on Saunders paper

47/33 cm ,by Victoria Sara Dazin

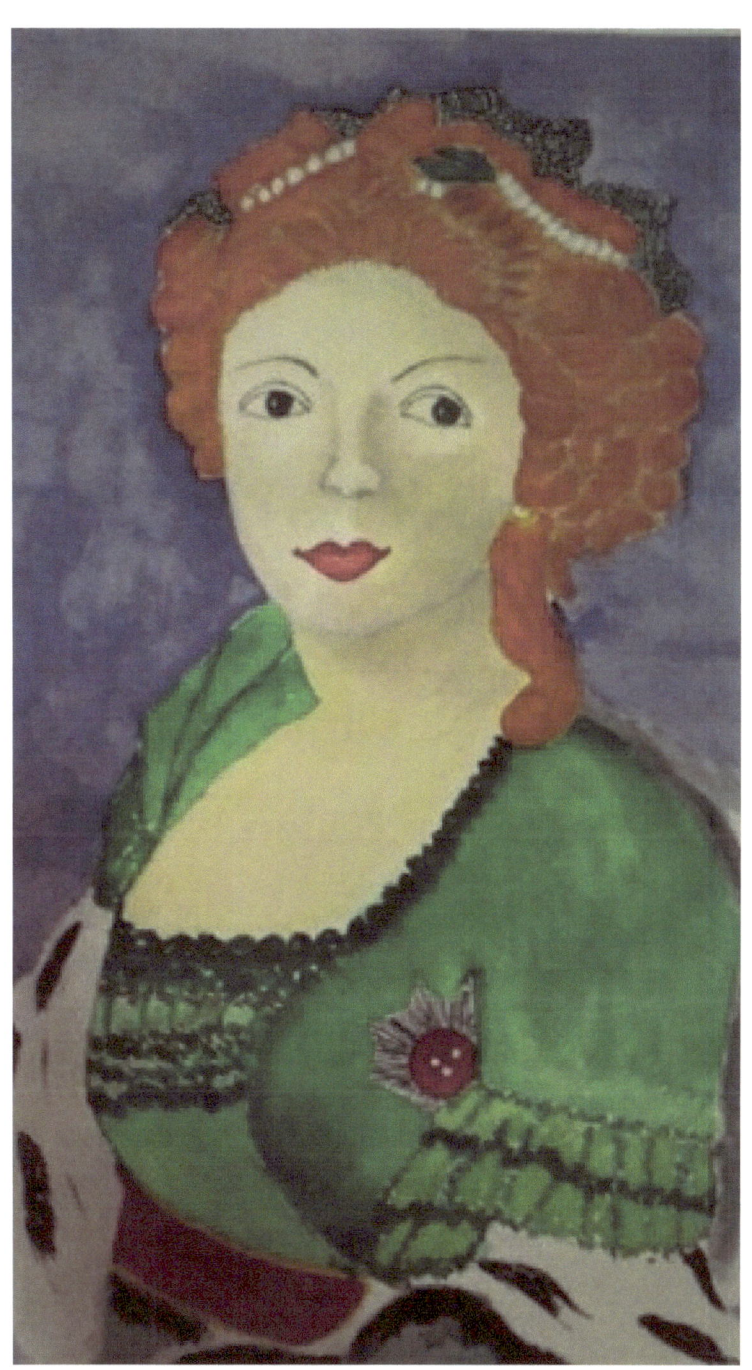

Young woman

aquarelle on Saunders

paper 47/33 cm,by Victoria

Sara Dazin.

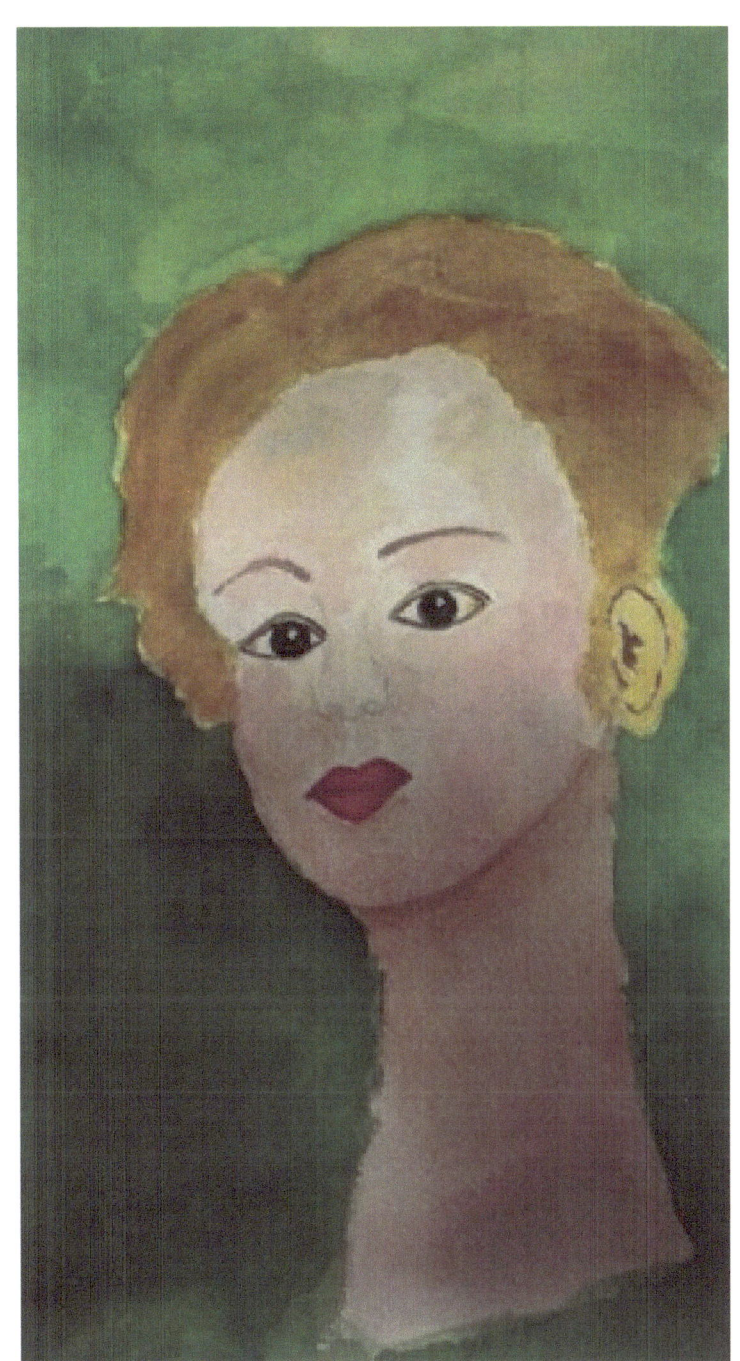

American young woman

aquarelle on Saunders

paper 47/33 cm,

by Victoria Sara Dazin

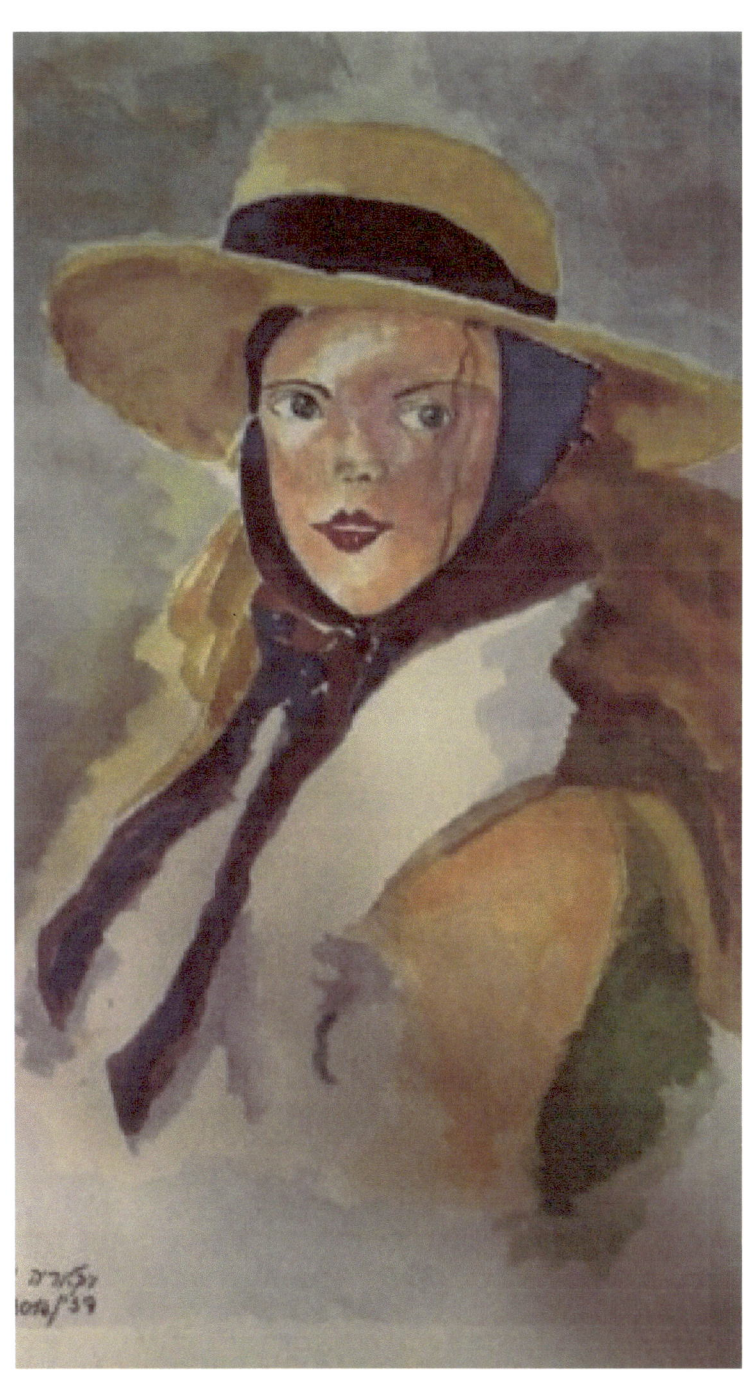

אלואה' "
100/'39

!HAG PESAH SAMEAH

יציאת מצרים

Aquarelle by Victoria Sara

Dazin, on Saunders

paper 55/26cm.

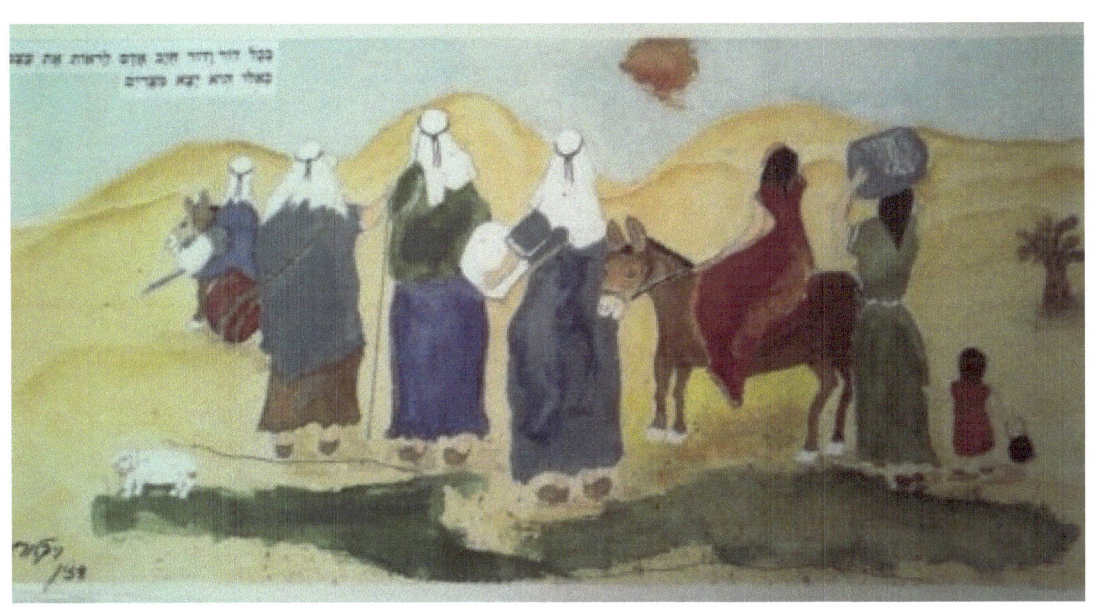

A pair of cranes in Hokkaido

by Victoria Sara Dazin

Water color on Saunders paper

425g/m2, 46/30 cm.

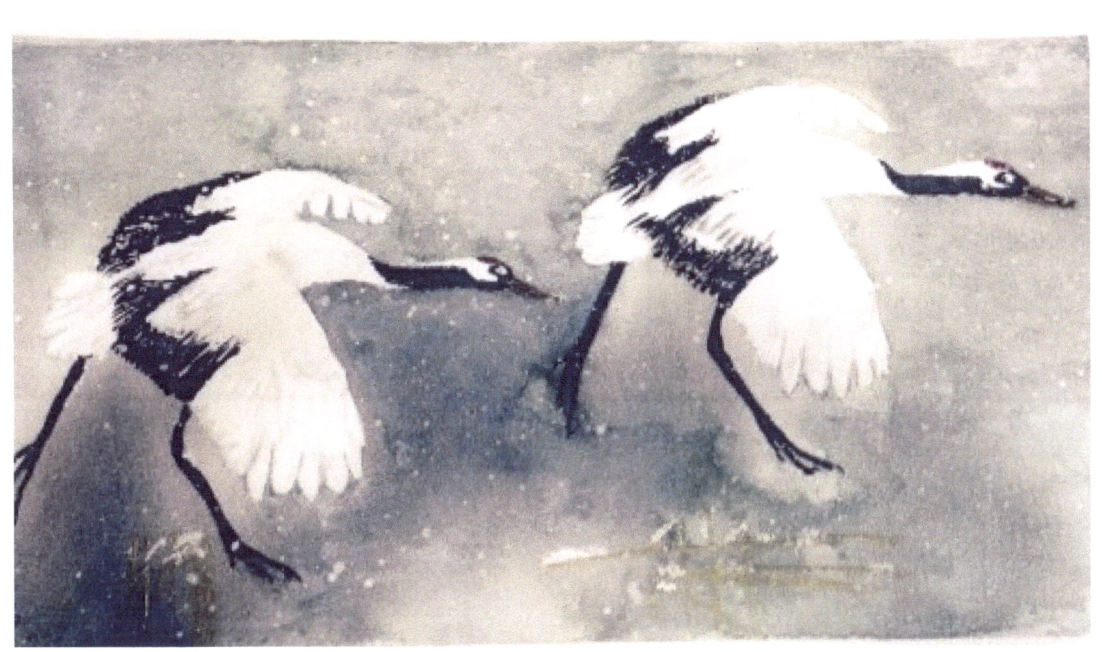

Vermilion Falls by Victoria Sara

Dazin .Water color

on Saunders paper, 47/32 cm.

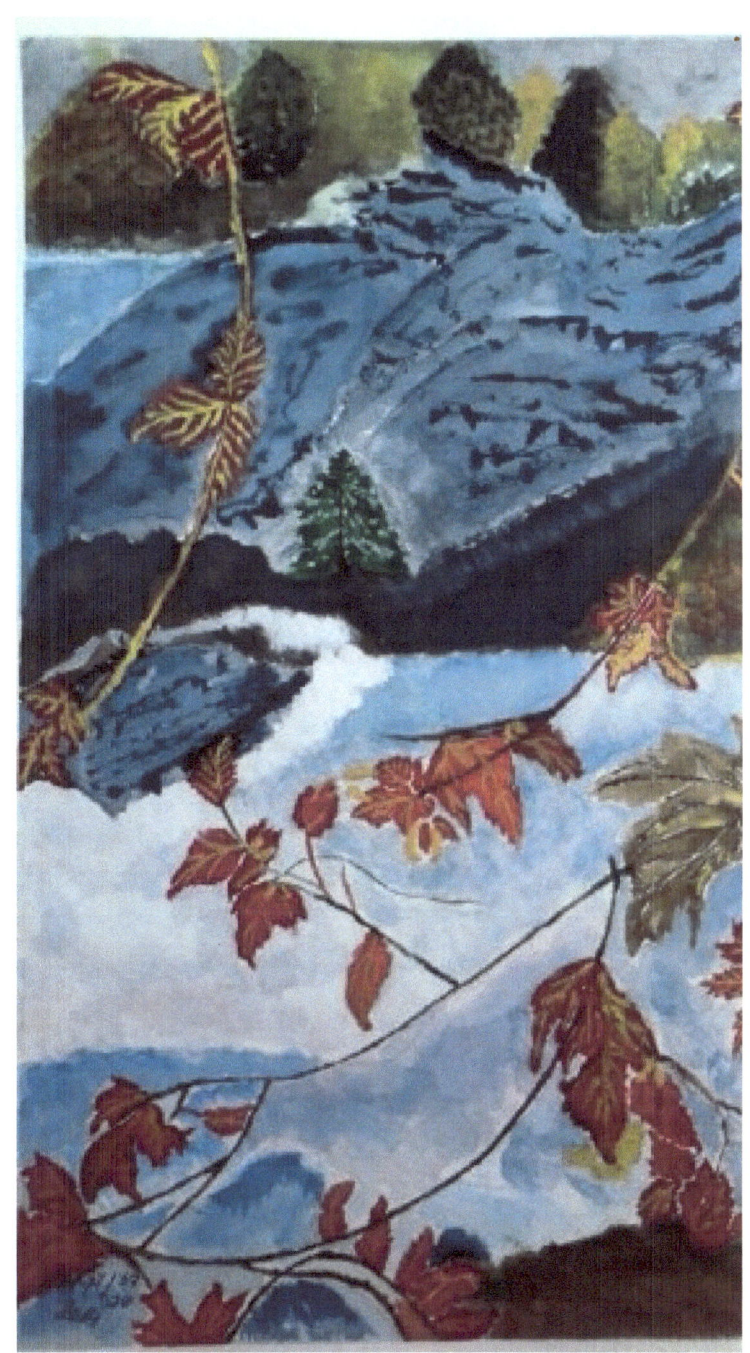

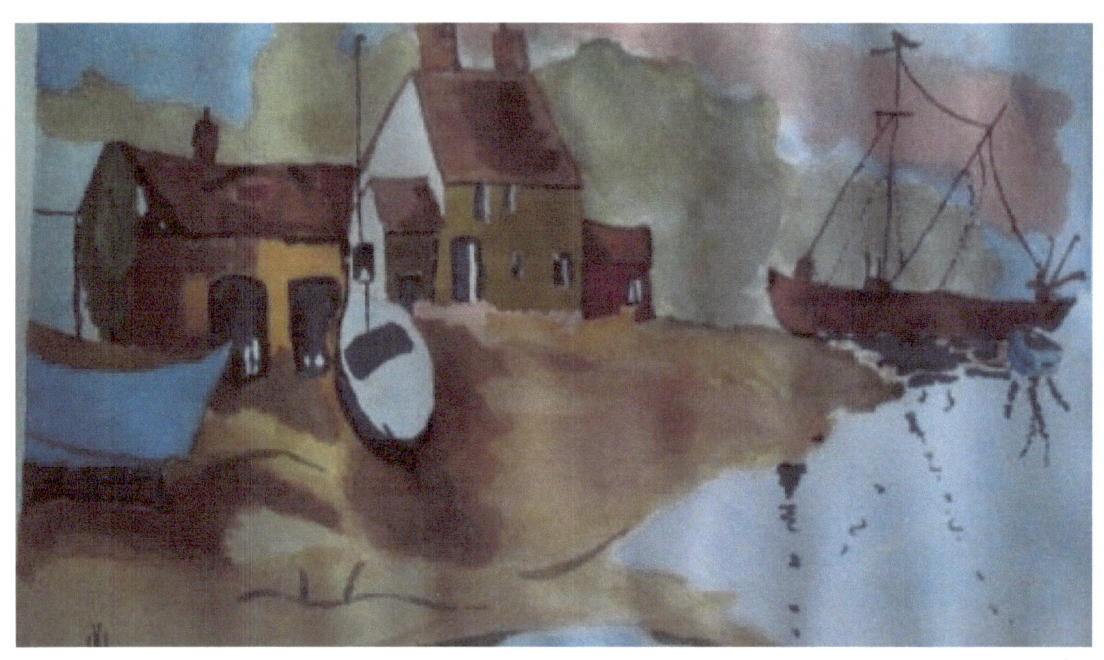

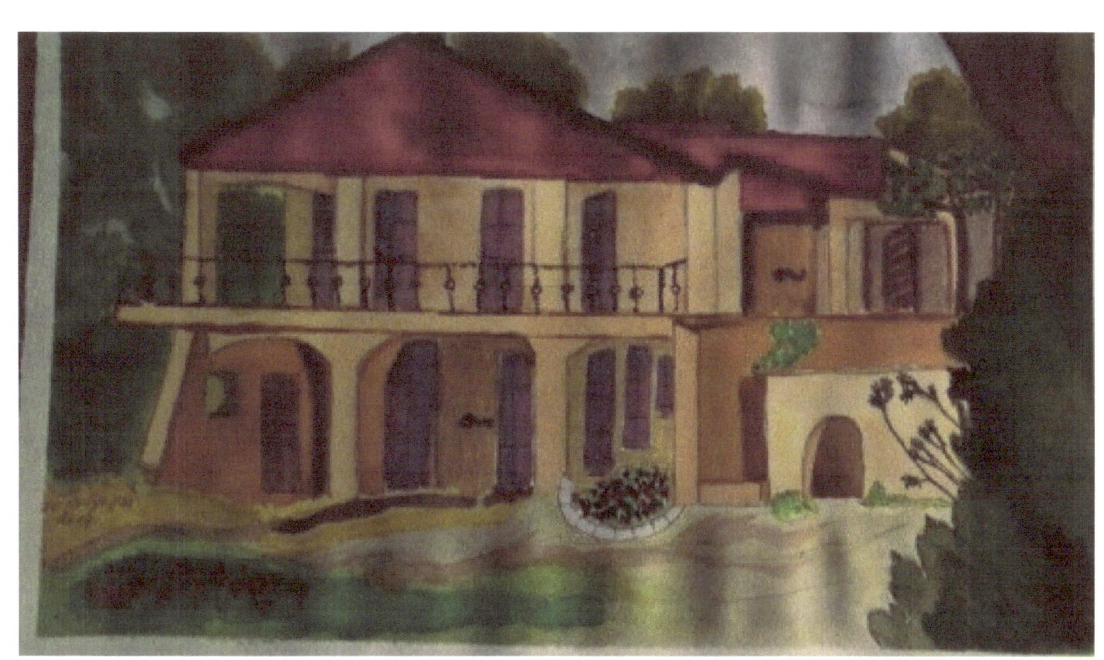

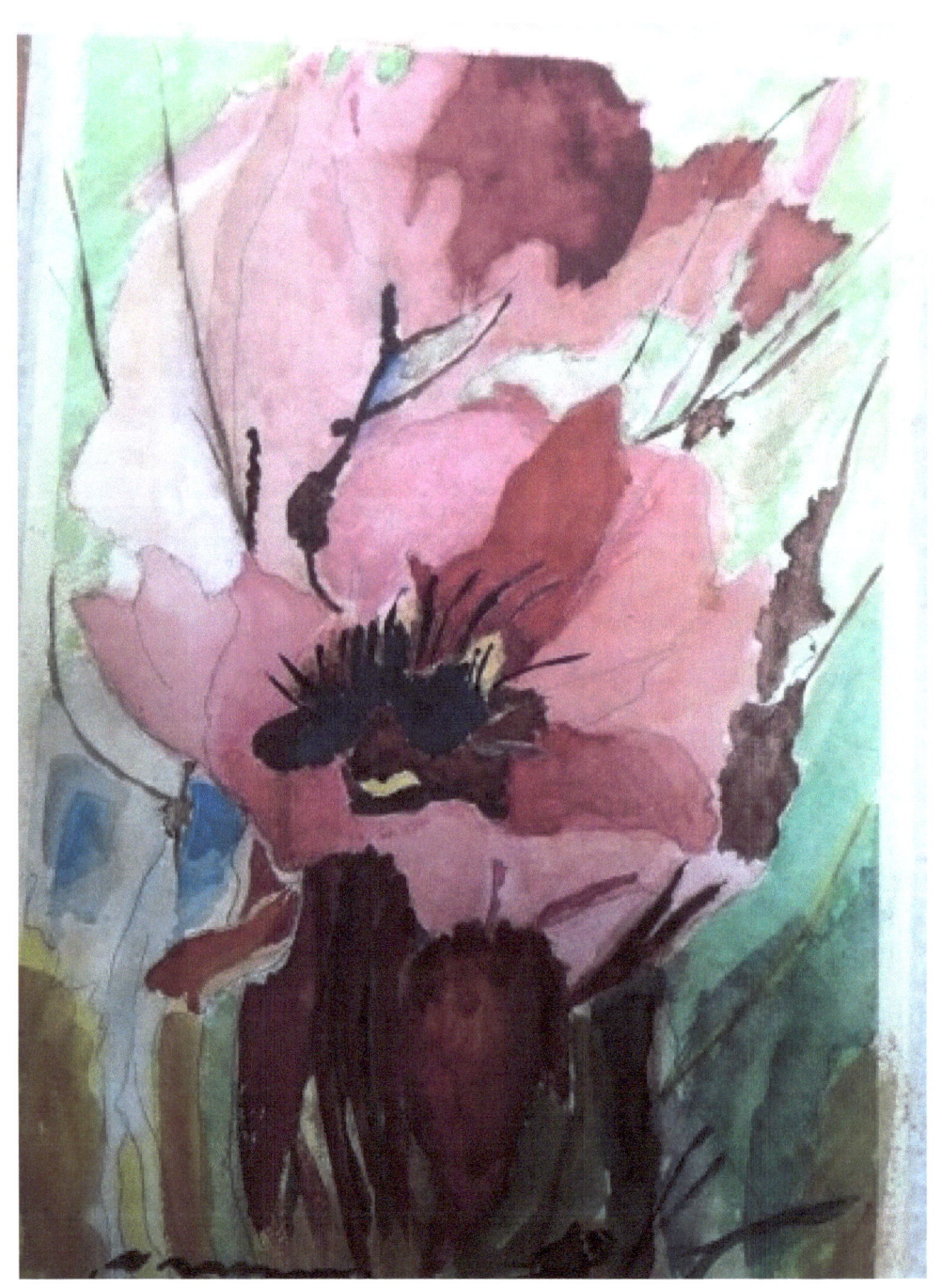

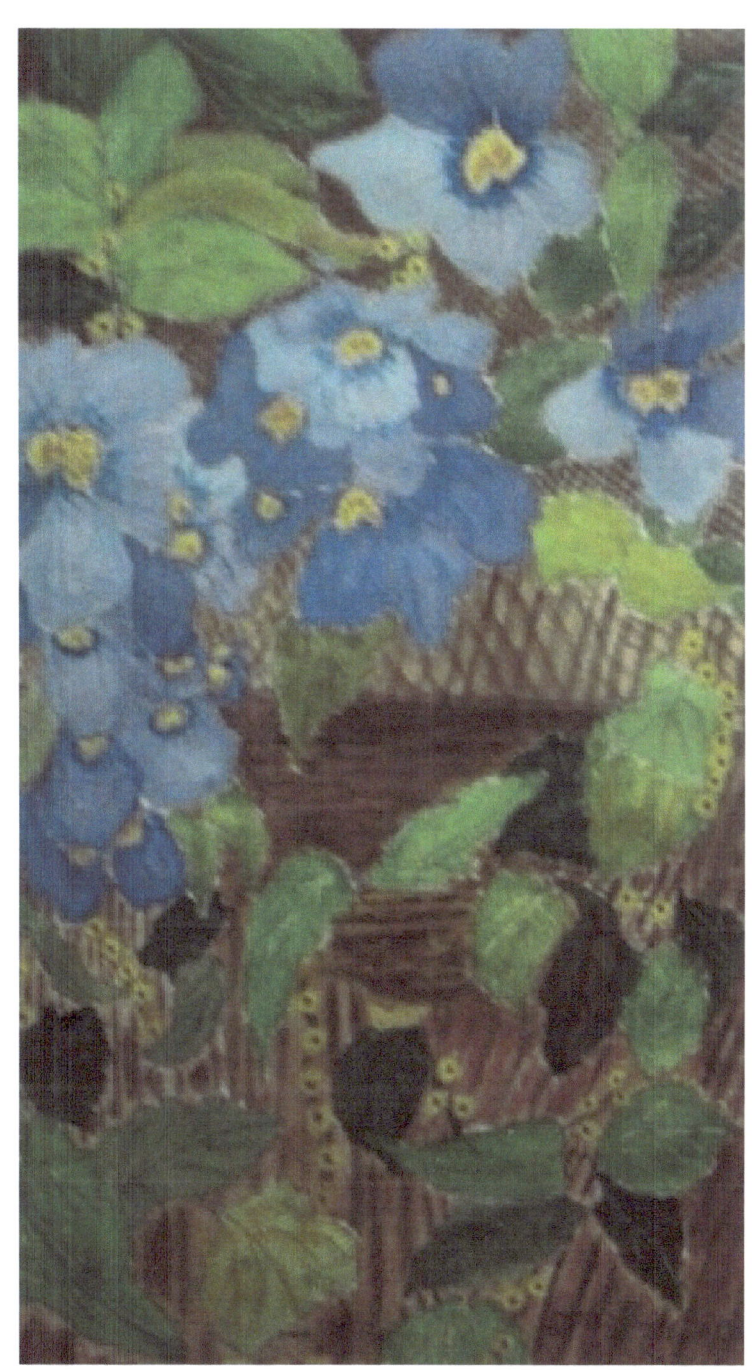

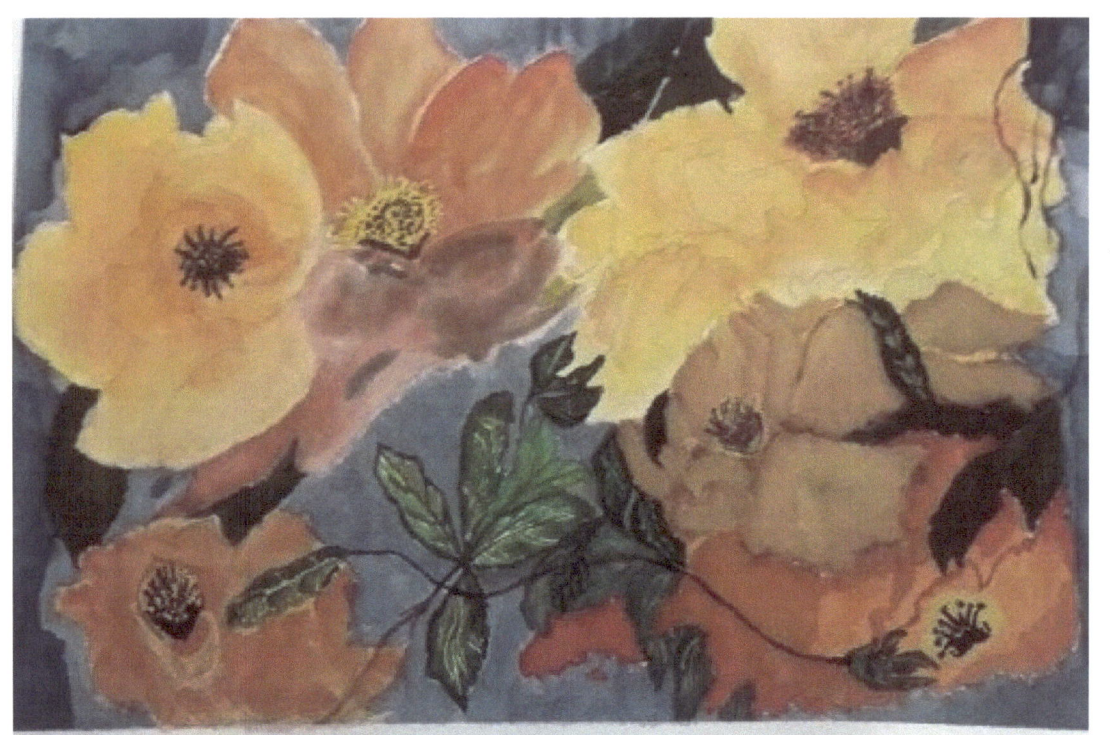

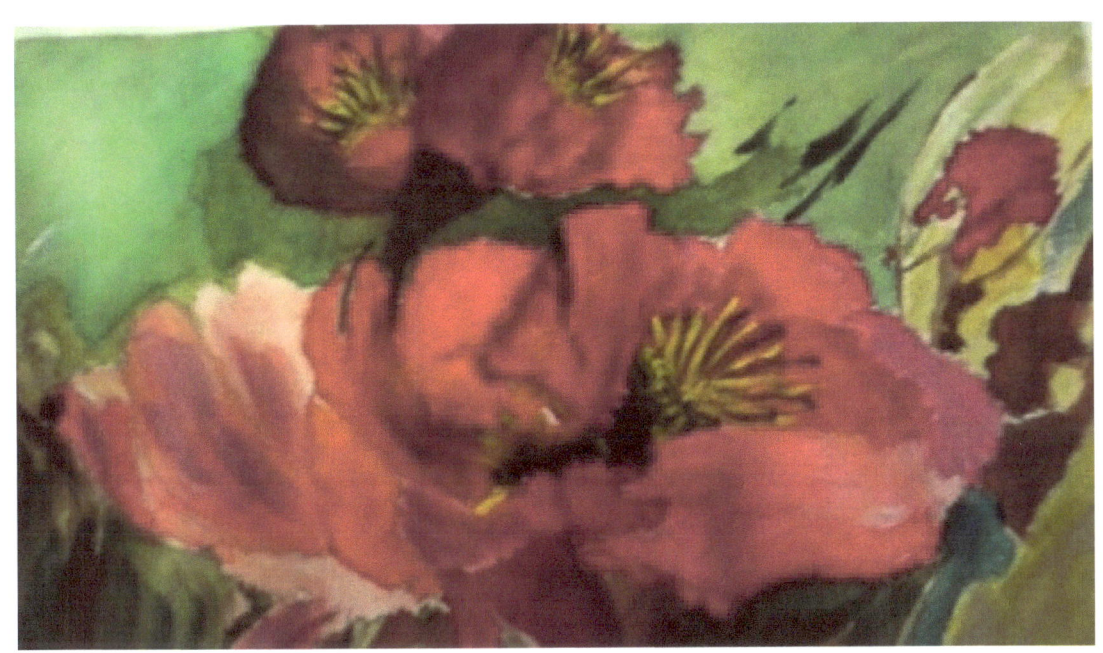

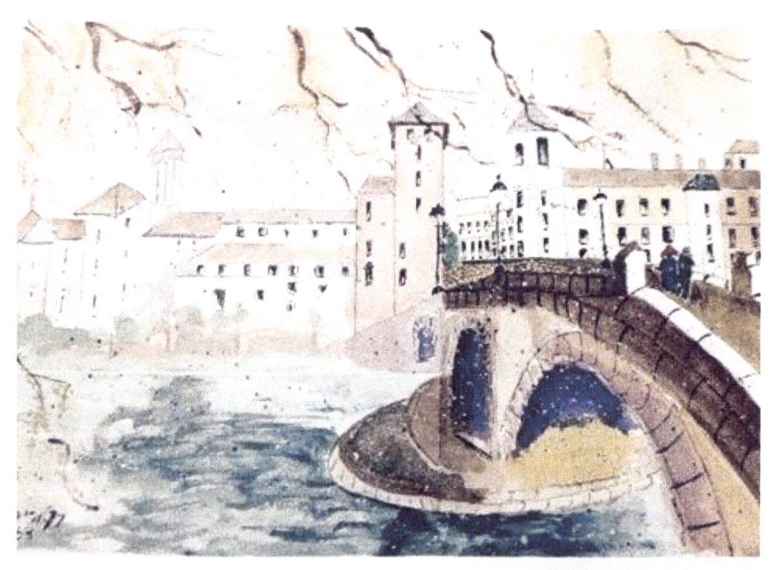

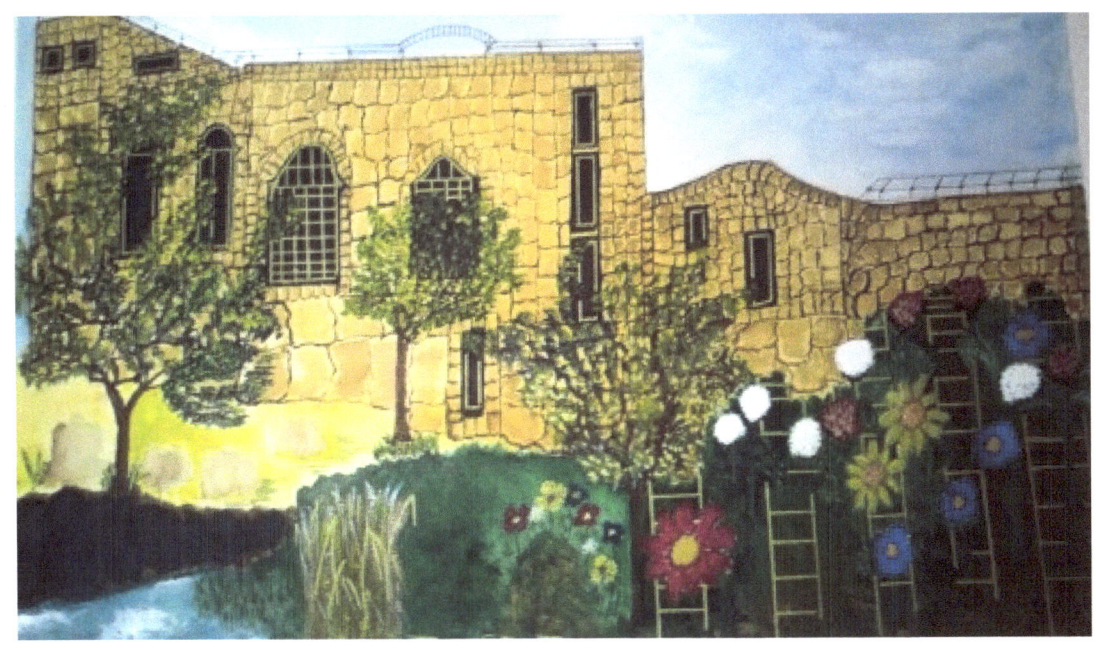

)